Principled Headship

A Teacher's Guide to the Galaxy

Revised Edition

Terry Mahony

Crown House Publishing
www.crownhouse.co.uk

First published by

Crown House Publishing Ltd
Crown Buildings, Bancyfelin, Carmarthen, Wales, SA33 5ND, UK
www.crownhouse.co.uk

and

Crown House Publishing Ltd
P.O. Box 2223, Williston, VT 05495-2223, USA
www.CHPUS.com

© Terry Mahony 2004

First edition published 1999
Revised edition published 2004
Illustrations © Les Evans

British Library Cataloguing-in-Publication Data
A catalogue entry for this book is available
from the British Library.

ISBN 1904424309

LCCN 2004100557

Printed and bound in the UK by
J W Arrowsmith Ltd, Bristol

Contents

Acknowledgments

This book has its origins in the learning I gained in walking along-side my teachers, Stan Putnam, Dave Marshall, Ian McDermott and Robert Dilts; and its development in working with many Hampshire teachers. In finishing it, I drew on the experience and advice of my colleagues in the Education Department. I thank them all.

I have written this book with Walt Disney's words in mind:

"I would rather entertain people in the hope that they will learn, than teach people in the hope that they will be entertained."

Author's note

When I wrote the first version of this book, it was because I wanted to remind myself of the foundations of my original motivation to become a teacher. The final two decades of the last millennium had witnessed the rise of the competences curriculum for both teachers and students, and of improvement (output) targets for schools. Combined with procedures for quality assurance, I feared that the education of young learners would be staffed with teacher-technicians working within a factory school. I wanted to revive Lawrence Stenhouse's dictum that education was a *moral* enterprise, which, for me, means schools have to be values driven. John Elliott (1991) descried the fact that the professional competence of educators was being defined as mastery of pedagogical techniques rather than a mastery of the self in the service of expressed professional values. The framing of competences for teachers results from an (understandable) emphasis on the cognitive aspects of teaching and leadership and is therefore weighted towards the thinking skills. I drew attention to the missing domain of the affect – of the emotion. Daniel Goleman's many writings on emotional intelligence have helped restore the balance between the cognitive and affective domains, so that more leadership training now explicitly explores the related skills base of the 'soft' skills of being a head teacher.

After accompanying a group of teachers on a study visit to a school in a shanty town just outside Cape Town, a member of the group remarked that the visit "provided me with more learning and self-reflection than many of my past planned educational goals and targets. It re-affirmed my beliefs in people as wonderful human beings, in education as the best of the creative professions and provided me with some of the funniest, saddest and most memorable moments of my career." He had had his core values and beliefs revivified as he saw the teachers in that school live them in their teaching. Values that had, in his own country, got obscured by the demands for relentless improvement, by the imposition of national curricula targets, external assessment and competitive league tables. The political, social and economic challenges facing educators in the Cape Town schools are huge. They were matched only by the commitment of the teachers to do the best they could for their learners for the betterment of the wider community and the future of the country. For everyone in the group, therefore, the emotional impact of the visit outweighed our educational intentions. Our experience reawakened in each one of us, our original cognitively constructed educational values, our commitment to our own learners and a pride in the abilities of ourselves as professionals and the whole enterprise of the education of young people. The expression of such large-scale values is totally in keeping with Csikzentmihalyi's (2002) findings on how to achieve 'flow' in your life.

Those pressures to meet local and national targets are greater once you become a head teacher. So a question for you may be how, right from the first day in the post, do you resolve the conflict between being yourself and conforming to the expectations you think others will have of you? If you fail to resolve this struggle successfully, you run the risk of playing roles and adopting behaviours that are alien to who you are and ultimately dysfunctional and damaging to the school. Carl Rogers (1983) asked can you, as a head teacher, "dare to be you"? That is, can you be, in his term, 'authentic'? That is, can you be true to yourself, your beliefs and values, and lead the school according to a clear set of principles? Can you walk your own talk? And in that talk can you express yourself sufficiently well as a person so that what *you are* will be clearly communicated?

In the Asian martial arts, you are exhorted to always move from your *dan tien*, your physical centre of gravity, the point just below your navel. This is the way in which you remain balanced in all your actions. More than a balancing point, the *dan tien* is seen as the centre of your physical and spiritual energy. My spiritual *dan tien* contains the set of core beliefs and values from which, like the physical centre, I draw my energy and shape my actions. As a teacher, I hold the belief that if I can teach anything at all, it is "I can teach what I am" – I can offer myself as a model. As a leader, can you behave in such a way that will be perceived by the school team as trustworthy, consistent and reliable? So that your behaviour will not be perceived as threatening, but liberating and empowering? I hope that this book helps you answer these questions for yourself.

However well-intentioned my aim in writing this book, it cannot give you the skills to be a good head teacher. What this book can do however, is open up your mental map and present ideas for you to reflect on, and experiment with, in your everyday life.

Preface

I don't know if this was your experience but when I was at school the teachers seemed like a different race to us. I think this was partly because I never had a sense of them as people who were learning anything or indeed had anything to learn. They were the teachers and we were the students. They were the dispensers of knowledge and we were there to be taught. Right up to the age of 16 when I left I never had a sense of them as being learners like us. Any idea of a partnership in which both parties were involved in learning would have seemed an extraordinary idea then. This segregation between those who knew (teachers) and those who didn't (students) reached its apotheosis in the view most of us had of the head. The head teacher, who in my school was known as the headmaster, was a figure of truly Olympian remoteness. He was a figure in a flowing academic gown seen from a distance – unless you had done something wrong, in which case you could expect an uncomfortably close encounter.

I first met Terry Mahony when he took his NLP Master Practitioner training with us at International Teaching Seminars in 1996. I knew nothing about his background but early on in this five month programme I recognised in Terry a really committed learner. Here was someone who wanted to know, someone in fact who was a trainer of teachers who was eager to learn and who I knew would then teach others. Since then I have seen him in a number of our other NLP programmes. What has impressed me is how he has taken what he has learnt in each of them – the training, consultancy and health programmes – into the education field.

There is something enormously fulfilling in seeing your students go on to produce their own contributions to the field. In my home I have a very special bookshelf which has only books written by my students which they have given me. For me it represents a behavioural demonstration of a real learning partnership – what I guess I never really felt myself when at school – where the student is sufficiently empowered to make their own contribution.

My hope is that this book will further such learning partnerships between heads and those in their care. *Principled Headship* has an enormous amount to offer anyone who is in the very challenging position of being a head in any kind of educational establishment – actually in any kind of establishment. Its focus is both on the how tos but also on the beliefs and values which need to inform our behaviour if we are to be successful and fulfilled. That's why, in truth, this book is for anyone who is in a leadership role, who wants others to learn and grow – and who is not afraid to be a learner.

Ian McDermott

Foreword

The purpose of this book is to give you specific and usable skills in leading a school into and beyond the millennium. School improvement is the theme of this era. Head teachers are facing challenges previously unknown. I don't just mean the challenge *of* headship. I mean the challenges you will face *in* headship *about* your headship. Challenges to how you are leading the improvement of the school, at a national level from external inspection, at a regional level from local advisory teams and at school level itself, from an active and effective governing body. It would be good, wouldn't it, if all head teachers were sufficiently well skilled to lead improvement confidently? This book offers you a fresh and practical approach to how you can clarify and strengthen your inner beliefs and values so that your own leadership behaviours will develop subtly. It does this by providing you with a map of principles and beliefs covering the field of leadership in schools. As a map it allows you the freedom to design your own route through from where you are now, to even more successful leadership. It is also a manual to turn those principles into operation as it contains activities to explore changes in your own thinking, your own emotional awareness and management and your language. Together, these will, by the end of the book, promote changes in your own behaviour to make them more congruent with your beliefs. With the changes you make will come higher levels of personal effectiveness through the greater motivation and co-operation of your staff.

It has been arranged as a sandwich – a packed lunch for a journey. Part Two, the filling at its centre, provides the material for your future growth and development into a healthy person. It is a practical guide to developing the skills that will make your practice of headship more satisfying. It is based on the belief that you have the capacity to attain your goals and enjoy fully being a head teacher. Don't read this part of the book unless you want to change, for it can change how you think and behave in a way that will bring you new achievements as a leader. The outside slices, Parts One and Three, are as fundamentally honest and nutritious as bread. You can consider them as wholemeal if you like because they contain kernels of protein that are linked to the filling and therefore complement and balance the centre.

"This guide is definitive. Reality is frequently inaccurate."

Douglas Adams
The Restaurant at the End of the Universe

Introduction

"Education is… a journey into the infinite, a participation in the movement of the universe"

Herman Hesse

"Beam me up, Scotty"

How often have you wished you could use Captain Kirk's famous phrase to follow his example and fly away from an alien, threatening form of life in an inhospitable school? To feel the relief of rematerialising in the warm safety of your own familiar mother ship? As a head teacher, facing the unknown wonders of the future, where is that special place? Where will your security lie?

Isn't the best place in your own principles, your own beliefs and values?

If you think you can answer 'yes' to that question, then the next question to ask yourself is:–

What principles guide my behaviour as a leader?

Since your principles are the launch pad of your behaviours, articulating your principles to yourself links your language with your behaviour. Scientists claim that of the 80,000 thoughts you typically have today, 60,000 will be the same thoughts you had yesterday! This is because you live most of your life on automatic, following long-established patterns of behaviour. In a similar way to a computer, our complex behaviour in everyday contexts is based on many, much simpler, programmes at a deeper level. These behavioural patterns are established in the neural pathways of our mind and are evidenced in our speech. The words we use give others clues to what sort of pre-programmed patterns are going on inside us. Conversely, our speech and behaviour can develop and reinforce such neural programmes. The study of how language and action affects the central nervous system is known as neuro-linguistic programming. It was first developed by John Grinder and Richard Bandler (1975) who studied transcripts of the language of acknowledged leaders in the field of conversational therapy. Behind their classification of the language patterns used by these models of excellence, they uncovered similarities in their thinking and belief systems. This is the work that gave rise to many of the principles in this book. They come from current ideas about how you form your own individual beliefs and how you sustain those beliefs in your daily living. Out of this study has come a range of techniques and procedures designed to allow you to develop your own inner resourcefulness and achieve your goals.

There are many writings describing successful heads. They are the results of research studies linked to theories of leadership or case studies of excellent head teachers and have titles like *'the eleven characteristics of an effective head'* or the *'eight attributes of great leaders'*. They are good guides of *what* to look out for and aspire to. They don't usually tell you how to acquire and develop them. These attributes and characteristics hang in the air in front of you, like the grin on the Cheshire Cat: appearing, appealing to you and then disappearing, leaving you wishing you could see the whole cat – and grab hold of it. The problem is, as Alice remarked as she wandered in Wonderland, "I've often seen a cat with a grin, but a grin without a cat? It's the most curious thing I ever saw in my life". It seems to me that many management books are collections of such grins. A guide has to be more than a list of external features. It has to utilise the modelling process of Bandler and Grinder. This book describes a set of internal beliefs, which work outwards, allowing you to shape yourself into the best leader that only you can be as the first step in that modelling process. It offers a way of linking the studies of excellence with your own daily management actions.

Education is a people enterprise and relationships are the key to the successful accomplishment of its primary task of pupil achievement. People are the school's primary resource. There is no school improvement or curriculum development without people development. The quality of interpersonal relationships – between staff and between staff and pupils – is the greatest single factor in the development of the school as a learning community and therefore of gains for all its students. It is the relationship between teacher and learner, not the technical skills of teaching, which are the strongest determinant of what a child learns. In the same way, what ultimately helps or hinders the improvement of a school is the relationship between the head and the individual member of staff, not the technical skills of management. That is why this book focuses on those key principles that are the basis for building good relationships with and between people.

Imagine what it would be like to lead a school that really works, where you have all the time you need to do the things you want and have the respect and co-operation of your staff as well as the support of all the parents. A school fit for children. That would be like heaven, wouldn't it? But how do you get to the heavens? Sylvia West, a head teacher in Cambridge, began by posing, to her colleagues, two vital questions in 1993 about being a head:

"What values will you/did you bring to headship?"

"How will you attempt to realise these values in the practice and organisation of your school?"

This book offers some answers to both those questions, because it is a compilation of the distinctive guiding principles that many head teachers and other managers have found to work in the daily round of leading a school team towards its goals, to reaching its chosen stars. According to the Collins dictionary, a belief is 'a principle accepted as real or true' and a principle is 'a standard or rule of conduct'. The principles in this book conform to these definitions.

Valuing is a basic human process. Each one of us expresses preferences and antipathies for certain people, certain situations and occasions. These preferences, even if not well articulated, determine what we are drawn to and what we shrink away from; what we desire and what we reject. As you visit many different schools, it is easy to detect differences in their atmosphere, culture and ethos. This is not surprising, as they all reflect and sometimes magnify, the values of their individual community. And head teachers, like the communities they lead, have different values, which take expression in the feel of the school and are therefore easily detectable to an outsider. This is because values are defined by the visible behaviour. The ringing words in a school prospectus can sound off-key if they are not lived out in the school by its community. To answer Sylvia West's question you need first to describe your values to yourself and then think about their realisation in action. The principles of this book are based on values which can be operationalised as behaviours, through the selected activities. You can clarify your values by doing the activities.

However, you may not think you can believe all these principles yet – this does not matter. Take the ones you can believe and live them. For the others, when you are ready, act as if you do believe them, because a personal value remains a whisper in your mind until it is put into practice. Watch what happens as you do. They may feel strange at first, as you will find the changes in your relationships interesting. Listen to what others say around you and judge their effectiveness for yourself.

Journey into space

When did you last see the full glory of the night sky? Even if you live in a small village, it is difficult to get a sight of the sky that is totally free of man-made lights. Take time to find a place and a night and treat yourself to the view. You can see just how bright the starlight can be, how many different sorts of stars there are, the Milky Way in all its magnificence. For the Celts, the stars were so many holes in that fabric created by warriors breaking through to the heavenly light at the centre of the universe. You can let your mind travel deeply into the darkness and the brightness of that space. I think of education in these universal terms – such a rich bluey-blackness, setting off so many jewelled lights. I have chosen that space, and its exploration in fact and in fiction, as the theme for this trip into headship, because like all teachers I know the value of a good story in promoting learning. You may recognize your own galaxy in it somewhere.

In voyaging around your galaxy, I hope you will find that this book is more like Dr Who's Tardis than Captain Kirk's Starship Enterprise. Like a Tardis, it may sometimes sit oddly in its landscape – small and not quite in the right place or time. On opening it up though, you can see that there is far more to it than first meets the eye. Instead of a telephone booth space, there are many rooms all equipped with the latest neuro-linguistic technology. A proofreader said to me that's why the language and syntax used in this book sometimes sounds quirky. If, like her, you are a native English speaker, it will just sound unfamiliar, but you will be surprised how easily you will get used to it. Preparing for university in the 1960s, I wanted a career in rocket science. It was *the* business to be in. There was no more exciting, ground-breaking technology; it was literally white-hot technology and would shape the future of mankind. I think of neuro-linguistic programming (NLP) as human rocket science for the next decade. And just as rocket science is now commonplace, so too will NLP be as it is incorporated into initial teacher training. For teachers have the most to benefit from its applications in the classroom. Also, unlike rocket science, the technology of neuro-linguistic programmes is easier to understand and use. It links what we know about the neurology of our body, mind and senses, with our verbal (and unspoken) communication patterns to help us better understand our thinking and behaviour patterns. As you use the technology – the practical programmes of action – to gain that understanding, to explore your own experience and what you do with it, you can bring about change and more personal effectiveness in your role, in your own professional mission as a school leader.

Captain Kirk had a mission "to boldly go..." What is your mission as a head? What guides your behaviour? The Teacher Training Agency may not have used the word mission, but it has defined the 'core purpose' of headship as:

"To provide professional leadership for a school which secures its success and improvement, ensuring high quality education for all its pupils and improved standards of learning and achievement."

How you fulfil this as a head teacher will be governed by your values and your personal vision.

As you may know, the Tardis allows you to travel in space and time. So does this book. As you read it, you may find yourself returning to parts of your own past universe – to where your values spring from, or where your beliefs developed, but its main purpose is to take you forward, "to boldly go" into the future.

Live long and prosper!

Part One

The extent of the known Universe

Planet Headship

Unlike Captain Kirk you are not exploring for exploration's sake. You have a destination in mind – headship. What would a map of this, your destination planet, look like? What sort of terrain will greet you on arrival? In the 1960s as we planned to reach the moon, debate raged as to whether the dust covering of the moon would be a few millimetres thick or several metres. Everyone wanted assurance that the landing spot would be solid and stable and not like quicksand. How do you ensure your chosen landing site is safe?

What is headship territory? Has it got a recognisable topography? Who has drawn a map? In the 1990s the British Teacher Training Agency drew up the first map of what it saw as the basic landscape of headship – the National Standard for Headship. Its National Professional Qualification for Headship (NPQH) is a classification of the attributes, skills, knowledge and task areas of headship. It listed eleven leadership skills, five communication skills, four self-management skills and three decision-making skills. The knowledge and task areas are well defined, but the relationship skills are not. Here the map gets fuzzy. And yet it is these that will ultimately determine how well you accomplish the overall task of leading a school. Also, although the standard appears comprehensive in terms of a job analysis approach to headship, it provides a higher level of detail than you may need at the beginning of your journey. Like most people, you may be able to hold only about five to seven things in your head at any one time and the principles in this book number more than that. So they are grouped into just five skill areas, based on you as a person, rather than on you as a conceptual model of a leader. In its Ninth Report (1998) the British Parliament's House of Commons Select Committee stresses "There is no single ideal model of school leadership" and goes on to add that "Good head teachers share common values and skills, and the relative importance of different attributes will vary according to the circumstances of individual schools". This book is a selection of those common values and skills and you can see how they are linked to part four (*Skills and Attributes*) of the National Standard:

You	*This book*	*NPQH standard*
what you sense	awareness skills	Leadership skills (a)
what you feel	emotional skills	
what you think	analytical skills	Decision-making skills (b)
what you say	linguistic skills	Communication skills (c)
what you do	behavioural skills	Self-management skills (d)

The gap is obvious! However, more and more attention is being paid to a head teacher's emotional skill and resilience. Although not directly tackled in the NPQH training programme, within the final assessment for the award of the NPQH more emphasis is now put on the personal attributes – the beliefs and values aspects of the standard. As we begin the second millennium, Daniel Goleman's ideas on emotional intelligence began to impact on leadership thinking and some of it has appeared in related training programs. Few, however, translate his ideas into exercises in developing the skills of emotional intelligence. The NPQH standard has now been revised and redefined as six areas of leadership learning which are intended to capture "the essence of a head teacher's roles and responsibilities":

1. Creating the future
2. Leading learning and teaching
3. Developing self and others
4. Managing the organisation
5. Promoting professional accountability
6. Building community through collaboration

How much more dynamic these areas sound! How much more motivating!

More importantly for the theme of this book, each of the six areas contains a list of Personal Qualities, every one of which, contains statements of beliefs and values critically important to headship today.

Getting your pilot's licence

 How do you persuade the educational inter-galactic high command that you are no longer a space cadet? That you have earned your wings and that you can take charge of your own mission ship? There is a training programme to support achievement of the British qualification, with an assessment procedure to help you reach the passing-out parade. However, as it is a teaching programme designed with the test in mind, it reflects an inevitable lop-sidedness between task and relational skills. It is obviously more time-consuming and more difficult to assess and train for the interpersonal skills dimension of being a leader. In 1983, Donald Schon described the problem space of leadership as being a high ground in the middle of a swamp. On the dry land, the problems you meet are technical ones and can be solved by systems, structures, planning and a defined agenda. Down in the marsh, the problems are about relationships, values and beliefs, all of which are unstructured and messy and demand more intuitive solutions.

As a teacher you have become good at intuitive solutions. They are part and parcel of the classroom as you intervene in people's learning. Part (e) of the standard begins *"Head teachers draw upon the attributes possessed and displayed by all successful teachers in the context of their leadership and management roles..."* and so acknowledges that you already have the mindset to be a leader. I start from that belief too and so the ambition of this book is modest – it aims only to uncover and make visible to you what you already know deep inside yourself. It is based on the belief that when you know what it is you know or can do, you become better at doing it. The development of personal and professional excellence in your own area of expertise and sphere of influence is the first of the five 'disciplines' or areas of learning described by Peter Senge (1990) as necessary for future leaders.

While some description of what is expected of head teachers is long overdue, it would be a mistake to think that the NPQH maps the whole world of what it means to be a head. A good atlas has a range of maps showing topography, climate, economics, population distribution and so on. The standard is the product of a particular view, one particular mindscape, of headship. It is necessary and it is informative, but it is far from enough if it is to embrace the full range of different potential headscapes. The danger of having a nationally agreed definition is that we may begin to think that only those that fit this one template are fit to be head teachers. Over-reliance on the standard alone could filter out the creative head, the idiosyncratic head, the challenging head and all those potentially great heads with the many, many different attributes not within the scope of the standard. We could in time, land on a planet of 'Stepford heads' of fully-functioning clones. Another drawback of a competency-based description of headship is that it cannot capture the wider social and political aspects of that position.

Recognising this, further national training for serving head teachers put together by the Hay Management Consultants examines the set of characteristics of highly effective heads mentioned earlier. These move closer to the principles of this book as they extend the list of skills and attributes into five areas to include:

1. personal values and passionate conviction
2. visioning
3. building commitment and support
4. information gathering for understanding
5. planning for improvement

More importantly their research on what heads actually *do* shows how these relate to each to give a profile of an effective head. They conclude that you do not have to embody all the characteristics – certain permutations of the eleven attributes combined into five areas can all lead to success as a leader. This would at least explain why very different types of people achieve success in headship. Successful leaders are not merely clones with all of the eleven characteristics. Recognising this, the National College for School Leadership is building on this sort of personal development approach, widening the opportunities for head teachers beyond the usual, narrow, instrumental management training to allow them to reflect on how their personal characteristics determine the quality of their leadership.

How would you characterise your life as a head teacher? The heart of this book is designed to provide you with a set of univers(e)al principles that will develop the fullest range of these desirable attributes. That is, attributes that are in the standard and those that are not, but from which you can choose those that are essential to making you the leader you are. More importantly, it contains a way of attaining and displaying those characteristics and answering that question for yourself.

Mindscapes and moonscapes

How many times have you heard that teachers should try working in the 'real' world? How many times have you thought you would like to enable the speaker to travel through the thirty different worlds that you visit during your every working day? If travel broadens the mind, then mind and space travel in the classroom certainly shrinks the conceit – the conceit of thinking that the only 'real' world is the one I occupy. You *know* there are many real worlds. Teachers spend their day exploring the alien worlds of their pupils, nurturing and developing the richness of the very individual ecology of each one. Developing your own mental landscape through reflecting upon and improving your own internal model of the world, while realising how it shapes your decisions and actions, is the second of Senge's disciplines. Supporting the development of the maps of others is a skill that a head teacher carries forward from the classroom. Knowing the energy put in by teachers to this same task, is it any wonder that the mindscapes of many of them get neglected and begin to look more like a deserted moonscape by the end of term? A head teacher has to carry this knowledge of multiple worlds from the classroom into the task of leading a school and be prepared to wander in the worlds of the school staff, whilst ensuring that they too gain refreshment and professional growth and continue to flourish, while sustaining their own.

It goes with the territory

Just what is the landscape of headship? Some of the features in the landscape have already been described by others – the head as professional leader, the head as chief executive, as curriculum leader, etc., and you could add more. However, the dominant phrase that has emerged recently is the head as problem-solver, because headship can be seen as a problem-solving activity in real time (all the time!). And by problem, I mean tasks to be done, rather than difficulties to be overcome. This distinction is important. For too long the education profession has been reacting to newly-set external targets from the back foot. David Leithwood and his colleagues think "a problem is any challenge or task or job to be done which requires thought (conscious or unconscious) and some type of action". (I will return to the interesting idea of unconscious thought later in this book.) Perhaps a more precise descriptor of the primary role is 'head-as-problem-(re)solver'. We need to regain the profession's proactive culture where teachers move towards the school's own goals, guided by an over-arching vision for the school, or a common sense of where the school is going, resolving its own issues as they arise.

Robert Dilts (1991) believes that if you are to be this second sort of problem-resolver, it helps to define as fully as possible the area and boundaries of the issue, to know as fully as possible its true extent. Some surface 'problems' are really symptoms of much deeper ones. Venturing into headship can be daunting because of the apparent vastness of the space involved. When astronomers look at a star they remain conscious of the space that lies around it, its gravitational field and its effects on the star. Equally important in headship when tackling a problem, is to be aware of the total problem-space you are in. How far it extends out, or up, or down. It is probable that each problem a head faces has a right answer – somewhere. It is more likely that each problem in practice has a multitude of answers rather than a uniquely true solution. These multiple answers are all to differing degrees, right; and all to differing degrees, wrong. There is no uniquely correct answer. Often, the problem-resolving skill specific to headship is to find the answer that is more right than wrong in your bit of space and time. And the first key to that is to know what planet you are from and the beliefs and values you bring from it. The second is to have the professional courage and integrity to deploy them in problem resolution.

What planet are you on today?

What the world looks like to you depends on what gets through the filters of the beliefs you hold in your mind and body, and what you have constructed from all the information that finally gets into your consciousness. Each one of us builds up a world picture that fits our beliefs and values and experiences and answers the questions we ask ourselves about the world. From these, we create a mindscape, an internal planet! In the face of many individual realities the belief to remember is that if there is only one right answer, then it's probably the wrong question to be asking.

Just as our selection of radio and TV stations determines the sort of music we hear and the pictures we see, the landscape we live in depends on what we tune into. Tuning into one station means tuning out of others. We actively filter them out from all the many channels open to us. The activity 'Filters of the Mind' in Part Two will help you identify some of your habitual preferences. It is based on some identified approaches to information that seem to be common in the population. If you know what your preferences are, you can realise that what you see and hear in the world around you is what you tune into. It's like shining a torch in the dark; you see only what the spotlight falls upon. Once you know that you prefer certain directions to others, you can choose to change and move the spotlight onto areas you normally keep in the dark. You can explore your own mindscape and understand how to reveal some of its hidden features through the principles and exercises included in this book. You can bring to the surface assumptions about your way of seeing, that you have been unaware of. More importantly, you can now become more sensitive to the filters of others.

Peter Senge provided a name in 1990, which we could appropriately choose for the name of today's planet headship – Metanoia – a Greek word for 'a fundamental shift of mind'. It's appropriate because the current job of the head teacher demands a different mindscape from even that of just five years ago. If you remain in that older mindset, you inhabit a dying planet.

Science fictions

If, like maps, your mindscape is your interpretation of the world, after you have filtered certain things out of it, how have you interpreted the differences you have allowed yourself to notice? How do you then describe your mindscape to someone else? The minute you use words, you begin a second layer of interpretation. You search for words to describe the image in your mind. Just as the map is not the territory, so your words are not the events you are describing. They are a distillate of all the words you could have used. They are both a précis and an approximation of the event. Because of the inadequacy of individual words you may resort to analogy, to metaphor. To that extent, though based on some fact, they are fictional stories. You may have legs like lead, a head buzzing with ideas – you may inhabit a school that is under siege that is like a sinking ship, just one happy family or forging ahead at full steam. How do you represent your school to yourself? How do other members of staff sense the school? Can you see the school as a brain – always active, always learning and adapting; as a prison – fenced around with constraints and restraints, with everyone counting off the days; as an ant colony, with everyone scurrying to play their part in its success? Such metaphors of organisations have very different effects on the people who work in them. Michael Lissack (1997) believes that "providing language and word choice is an essential managerial task" because the careful use of words is more likely to bring about productive staff than any amount of direct orders. This seems particularly true of schools.

Personal metaphors are just as powerful as organisational ones. How do you see yourself? Most heads adopt one or more of Carol Pearson's (1998) archetypes at different times in their journey. Sometimes the leadership task in the school needs an 'Orphan' head – bringing the gift of resilience to struggle through the current adversity; at other times a 'Warrior' head proving their worth in the achievement of the school's goals. And in 1997, David Loader described the phases of his leadership of his college in a similar way, by describing himself metaphorically as the alchemist-leader at one time, or as a Cinderella or as a dreaming leader at others. With each one comes a different story. And each story, each metaphor, brings with it different connections for you and for others.

If each metaphor, each story brings with it a whole host of different meanings and associations, then choosing the appropriate one may determine the particular name everyone gives to your planet. More importantly, changing the metaphor can bring new insights to the situation as your mind compares the different facets of the metaphor with the situation you are experiencing. So, creative use of metaphor and analogy can be really helpful in breaking the grip of habitual ways of thinking, of opening up the possibility of new and resourceful ways to tackle an issue. Telling a good story is an invaluable leadership skill. For Celtic bards, storytelling and teaching were the same thing – they were about what is and what can be. And in telling the story they were careful to respect and honour the past, but were very aware of the present whilst pointing the way to possible futures. You too, may need to develop a good store of tales – all with a common ending – a great school. Tales that predict the future and prepare people for it. Tell the appropriate story to the governing body – one that reveals to them the value that a supportively challenging governing body can bring to the school; to the parents – one of partnership in the development of their children through to adulthood; to the staff – of the power of a learning community; to the children – of what it is to be human.

Principled Headship

How many management courses have you attended in your career? To become an effective time manager, stress manager, decision-maker, meeting manager or team builder? Is your course folder full of notes on the useful techniques of these different aspects of management? Are you now able to say 'no', prioritise paper, prepare purposive agendas and run effective meetings? Have you now created a dynamic staff team? These are all useful techniques to master. They are all rational approaches to the development of essential technical skills of management. Such courses raise your awareness and knowledge of those skills that you may particularly need to develop and what you may need to practise back in school. How many have you never really taken on board?

How many of them are second nature to you now? Guy Claxton (1995) believes we often mistake knowledge (or know-what) for know-how. It is rational to think that if you are given knowledge, then know-how will automatically follow. The only problem with rational approaches is that very often the problems you face as a head do not have rational solutions. This is especially true of schools – if they had only rational problems, schools would be problem-free because we can all develop rational solutions to rational problems. Developing intuitional solutions to non-rational problems is a skill that can be learned.

We need well-organised schools to educate the young. We need skilled and well-qualified teachers. We may need educational structures like the national curriculum and school inspection. We certainly need skilled and well-qualified teachers. A scheme of national standards for all grades of teachers and school leaders is admirable and long overdue. But all of these are only part of the answer. Neither the management techniques, nor new organisational structures of themselves improve the quality of the teaching in the school – only people do that. And people do things for their own reasons; they are often irrational. A major drawback of government plans is that they assume that school improvement is a totally rational process, which can be gained by the construction of rational action plans. If it were totally rational we would have problem-free schools breaking out everywhere by now!

One of the reasons many of these techniques are not fully utilized is that they are seen as additions or extensions to current management *behaviour* instead of springing from a set of internally held *beliefs*. Trainers often do not link them with particular belief systems; trainees often do not consciously check the compatibility of these advocated behaviours with their current beliefs about headship. Like some teachers, managers can carry myths throughout their professional lives about effective practice, about what works, born out of a past specific incident or experience. Belief in these myths can inhibit further skill development. And beliefs are at a higher logical level of meaning than behaviour. So, often, it is at the belief level that change has to take place for newly learned behaviours to actually be employed back in school. Using a knowledge of neuro-linguistic programming, you can generate a particular set of beliefs and attributes pertinent to headship behaviours. They will form a core set of principles that will allow you to develop skills and techniques to help you resolve leadership issues using your own genius and resourcefulness.

How does a good head walk?

We all learn to walk by first imitating the adults in our life and fine-tune that copying through trial and error. We can use this technique of modelling ourselves on someone all through our lives. As adults we can do this more systematically than as infants. Like Bandler and Grinder, we can analyse the key components of a desirable behaviour. Separate them out and practise them singly. Then we can synthesise the set of behaviours, add our own special spin and practise them to our satisfaction. You can begin right now.

Sometime in your career, you have had the experience of learning something significant and lasting for yourself as a school leader, from watching or being with another person. Someone whose excellence in one aspect of their life you admired and wanted to emulate. Stop and remember now, what you saw and heard then. You can take some time now and...

...cast your mind back and see and hear that person again and recapture how you felt in their company.

For even as you are reading this you can realise now that there are other lessons to be learned from that experience in your past.

And when you have seen and heard something that you can now believe is of value to you, hear yourself telling yourself the same thing.

Imagine being like that now and in the future. Because then you can think of a situation that you know will arise within the next half-term... and notice how you can take this learning into this situation and realise that you are applying the new understanding from your past experience to increase your choices of action in the present.

A friend of mine, on getting his first offer of headship, leapt to his feet in delight to tell his colleagues the good news and then froze on the spot as the question at the start of this section arose in his mind. Just how *does* a good head walk? On the surface, it is an amusing, almost laughable question; at a deeper level, you can see that it is a really good question to ask yourself. At this intuitive level, he was looking through his memory for a good role model, one he could copy and carry with him into his future job. He recognised a grin that was worth having. But in order to copy it, he needed the rest of the cat around it. He had to create a picture in his mind's eye of the past colleague, so that, maybe, he could just feel the way he carried himself. Valerie Hall in her study of women head teachers found that they "worked with their own images of 'looking like a head' and 'being like a head'". My friend had used the same first steps into headship. Unconsciously he had rediscovered an important strategy for developing personal excellence – find a good role model and copy him or her. If he copied that walk, he too would be recognised as a good head and would be as successful as his mentor. We all began learning by imitation, by 'sitting with Nellie'. We now know that mimicking the person's external behaviour, is the first place to start, but it is not enough on its own to guarantee success. Knowing *what* they do is one thing; knowing *how* they do it is another. Modelling human excellence has become an accepted technology for teasing out the components of individual success and using them to accelerate the learning of another person. The usual modelling process explores four aspects of the role model:

- the beliefs they hold about their area of expertise;
- the values they espouse in working in that area;
- their mental approach or thinking steps, and finally
- their actual behaviour including the physiology they adopt.

Unpicking another person's thinking strategies is no easy task. But you can add to your copying of their demeanour or stance, with the two other strands of information. You can find out what it is that motivates your chosen models. What they value will tell you what drives them to do what they do. What do they believe about being a head? What does it *mean* for them? What do they tell themselves about themselves? What is important to them about being a head? You can get these pieces of information by just asking them such questions. Secondly, you will need to know how they experience themselves as heads – what do they feel like as they walk about, being a head? These strands taken together can be the start of the process of incorporating their excellence into yourself. This is one way to rebuild the cat around the grin that you remember.

In 1996, at the end of her research, Valerie Hall concluded that "the innate characteristics which may be relevant to being an effective manager and leader are not limited to gender". We shouldn't be drawn into thinking that there are specific leadership traits which are essentially female or male. Every leader has the capability to use the full range of possible behaviours shown by great leaders. External characteristics are often just the surface indication of some inner, deeper attribute – these are what are important. Through this book you can recognise and develop those inner qualities that result in the outwardly visible excellent head teacher. And you can be excellent. As Patrick Porter (1993) says in his guidance on becoming a genius, all you have to do is ask yourself "Is there a better way for me to act, to think, to feel, to be?". And if there is, be flexible enough to change. My head teacher friend said that "on a clear day, I can see management". And for you to see management and leadership clearly, you, like him, have to go deeper... into your inner beliefs and values.

Acting from the centre of your principles

The acting head

 In the ancient Greek theatre actors wore masks, pretending to be the character in the play. Some self-development books suggest actions which sound like the stage directions to an actor in a play – *walks upstage, waving hands; exit stage left, head bowed*. Marlon Brando is probably the most famous Method actor. He brought to everyone's attention the process whereby the actor started from the point of 'becoming' the character. Action and language then flowed from what it felt like to him to 'be' that person. Martin Scorsese describes such actors as "the real thing" because they become the other person for the duration of the scene. They do not need behavioural direction, for

once they have the feel of the person, once they have the right outlook and the appropriate mindset, the behaviour follows naturally. They can interact with the other characters. The sense of 'trueness' of those interactions makes such stage acting powerful. And it's the trueness and the congruence of a head teacher's interactions which makes them memorable. Personal and professional congruence is an attractor like a magnet – its truth draws other people to you, increases their sense of rapport with you and your influence with them. You may have recognised this in the attraction of the model you chose for yourself. When you interact in this way you have no need of masks.

As teachers, you know the value of coaching and building positive relationships. You have already identified one significant person in your career. Think of one of his/her characteristics that would serve you well. This book will help in acquiring that characteristic and growing it in yourself into success, because 'acting your way into thinking is easier than thinking your way into acting'. Acting is the first step in modelling – it may seem awkward and unnatural at first, but becomes learnt and then unconscious and therefore eventually 'natural' to you.

The centred head

Michael Fullan (1993) says *"the starting point for what's worth fighting for is not system change, not change in others around us, but change in ourselves"*. Fighting is a natural process if you consider fighting as facing the conflicts that everyday living puts in front of us. Fighting is not then the same as violence. There are many ways of fighting. Some of the Japanese martial arts are based on non-violence. Judo can be translated as *'the gentle way'*. Ai-ki-do as *'the way of blending energy'*, of not struggling against the energy opposing you. Accepting the energy; taking it and utilising it. This is a delicate balancing act and one that, like all judo moves, is taught through the repetition of small movements. Practised time and time again until they become unconscious and fluid. You are going to have tussles as a head – a myriad little 'fights' as you grapple with these day by day issues of leadership. Going through many small confrontations not only develops the ability to successfully face larger ones, it often prevents the slide into energy-sapping oppositional conflict.

What Japanese martial arts have in common with Michael Fullan is the store they put on mastery of your actions through your own self-management. A common skill in the different arts is that of achieving both an emotional and a physical balance. This is often taught through 'centring' – the ability to start all your movements from your centre of gravity, both mental and physical. This ensures that they are all harmoniously directed to the desired outcome. To stay on course as a head is often difficult, as the cross-currents of government targets, parental expectations and the needs of the students continually buffet your leadership. Under such forces the body prepares itself to fight or run away from the cause of the stress – you get knocked off course.

> I don't know if you can recognise the signs of these basic self-defence mechanisms in your own body – changes in your heart rate, your depth of breathing, the dryness or sweatiness of your skin and even the blood flow into your cheeks. You can notice some of them right now, even while you are reading this book. Probably, you are in a relaxed state. In that state...
>
> *Are you breathing high in your chest; or lower, from your stomach?*
>
> *Can you feel pressure on any of your leg and arm muscles?*
>
> *Is every inch of your spine comfortable, or is it twisted by the way you are sitting?*
>
> *Are your shoulders hunched?*

Ask yourself the same questions when you are in a noticeably different state – walking about the school or sitting in your office – and note and record the differences. Acquiring the habit of monitoring such things at different times in different activities allows you to notice differences and their effects on your body. Ignoring them for long periods results in the early symptoms of stress –

headaches, muscle tensions such as a stiff neck, skin complaints, more frequent minor ills, etc.

Remaining on course is helped by centring, by the skill of staying balanced around your centre of gravity. Physically, you can do this by standing with your feet slightly apart, resting your fingertips on your stomach, just below your navel, while deepening and slowing your breathing. Then close your eyes and become mindful of the principles that guide your action as a head teacher and letting these thoughts about what you want to happen, sink down to where your fingertips are touching. This physical centring is more than just a calming exercise, it is also a powerful way of staying emotionally, intellectually and professionally centred and in balance. It is a state of emotional and physical stability that you can choose to come into at any time, to manage the job stress of headship. Buddhists say that 'when the universe roars, only the heavenly dragon watches calmly and with delight'. I adopted the heavenly dragon as my badge of leadership with the aim of developing its skill of watching calmly so well in this centred state, that pure delight came soon after!

I cannot say that this book is the full set of principles describing the whole space of headship. I can say they are well-chosen principles, which together form a sort of neuro-linguistic aikido. Through centring and balancing and being mindful of the principles, you can marshal all your energies and resources to gain the outcomes you want.

The principled head

Martin Luther King represents for me a model for school leadership for the beginning of the next decade. He dreamt a vision that is now largely in place. He led people from the front by his example; from the middle, by standing amongst them; and from behind by inspiring and motivating those that came after him, to carry on the work of emancipation and fulfilment of that dream. And all this in following a strategy that could be described by both of the terms ju-do and ai-ki-do in that it was about confronting the status quo, fighting and 'toughing out' an opposing force and yet non-violent in its action. Some of the early tribes of the Americas would have recognised his 'four-hearted' approach. Whole-hearted in intent, strong-hearted in creativity with regard to strategy, clear-hearted about outcomes and open-hearted in action. You can bring about change in school even though you are not seeking a revolutionary change. You can model his behaviour, emotional centredness and strong belief system with regard to resolving the conflicts on the path to realising the vision of your school.

On a more earthly level, Roger Fisher and William Ury describe their strategy for negotiating successfully through disputes. They suggest that instead of arguing for and from your *position* on an issue, you are more likely to succeed if you act according to a set of *principles*. Their first principle is that you maintain at all times a keen desire to achieve a well-formulated outcome – an outcome that is good for all. There is no point in getting to a solution which, later on, becomes your next problem. (Most historians agree that the root cause of the Second World War was the negotiated settlement at the end of the First!) Their second rule is that you take an open-minded approach to all the options available to reach the outcome. And lastly, they suggest you have clear decision-making criteria. In the messy, swampy areas of headship, your beliefs and values are these criteria.

Over the last few decades, head teachers have been engaged in negotiating a stream of national and local initiatives into their schools. They have mediated the demands of a wide range of initiatives, from a centrally defined curriculum to target-setting, from financial management to value for money, from appraisal to the national standards for professional development. With more to come! Negotiating changes, whether from within or without the school is yet another key skill. Acknowledging that change brings conflict, accepting and taking responsibility for engaging with it and remaining flexible enough to do what it takes to resolve it, is the surest way to move forward. It's better than opposing or contesting it.

Acting in a principled way raises the question of just what are good principles for leading a school. The negotiating/mediating ones above occupy just one corner of the galaxy of headship. As a boy, living on a mountainside in Wales, I was fascinated by the night sky. Looking at the stars and reading about them, I wanted to move closer to them. I noticed at the time a strange effect. I was in the present, but the stars I looked at were, as I was seeing them, in the past. Their light had left them years before. Even stranger than being in the present and the past simultaneously, was the fact that all I could think about was the future! About space exploration and my part in it. I knew in my head that I was a small entity in a small corner of the universe. I also knew from my reading that those stars which I could see in the expanding skies, might just as well not exist, because, by now, some probably didn't. What seemed more important then was getting a sense of eternal verities, of universal guiding principles in my heart. I had discovered the first one. If I could conceive of infinity in my thoughts, then no matter what I thought I was – I was always more than that!

At that time, I adopted a medieval view of the world and assumed I *was* the centre of the universe – even if it was only my piece of it, my solar system – starting with me as its sun. Whilst I was an astronomer, my knowledge of space expanded as fast as space itself. The problem space of headship is large and, like the known universe, expanding annually. So large that sometimes it may seem daunting. But I knew that my mind was bigger than the universe. After all, I was able to 'experiment with infinity' inside the confines of my mind, to think about it all, inside my head. This was my first principle and it became the foundation of my whole set of principles:

I am more than I think I am.

The others grew from this. With a set of core principles and values, you can confidently explore your own bit of space. My core principles grew firstly in strength and only slowly in number. But they now fill my professional space.

The two-sided head

 This well-known diagram illustrates the mind's search for meaning (even where there is none) and its ability to focus on only one image at a time. You tend to see either the profiles of the two heads, or the chalice. You can switch between them, depending on which colour you decide is the background to the picture, and which is the foreground. Both can be either. This effect happens in all our perceptions. As we attach more importance to one aspect of an event so it moves into the foreground of our mind; and so other aspects fade into the background. Which we select as important to bring forward is often determined by the filters in our mind. These in turn are shaped by our past experiences and beliefs. The hubbub of a party is just background noise as we concentrate on the conversation we are engaged in. But your name will leap forward into your consciousness if someone in that background voices it, even when it is not directed at you and you will turn and look in the direction from which it came. Many times in school, the background noise grows and forces itself into the foreground. The head's task then often slides (and dangerously so) into the constant reaction to the many simultaneous conversations. Balancing the background and foreground so that the picture of the school stays in focus is the leadership role. To continually ask amidst the hubbub – "What is obvious here?" and "Does this relate directly to where this school is going?". To ask these questions entails stepping outside of the mêlée.

This is an aspect of the 'outside' skills of headship – that of being able to take another perspective – to see things from another's viewpoint, to feel what it might be like, standing in their shoes. It is an imaginative skill, a skill of invention and like all skills can be improved through practice. (See *Alien Views* in Part Two.) It's a way of getting two heads for the price of one – and both are inside your own head! Good solutions to resolving a problem come easier with the additional skill of bringing these two sides together so that both perspectives light up the problem area. It takes the two heads to see the Holy Grail that exists between them.

The inside-out head

Success begins inside, with:

- your view of who you are
- how you feel about yourself and
- what you tell yourself about yourself

That is, the 'inside' components of successfully leading a school are:

- clear understanding of **who you are** as a head teacher
- a set of **beliefs** geared to good performance in that role
- **values** that provide you with the motivation to put the time and energy into getting results both with people and for people
- **capabilities** that encompass the resources you need to do the job
- **behaviour** that is congruent with your beliefs and appropriate to the school and its community

What is your vision of yourself in and for a school? Taking a strong sense of personal vision into a school is the first condition for being able to co-create a team vision and the third of Senge's disciplines. To build a school community with a sense of self, a common identity which is robust enough to include the different individuals with their very individual differences within it. That demands a set of core beliefs and values that everyone can accept, which guide everyone's behaviour and actions towards making the vision a reality in terms of what happens to children.

Having looked into your inside head, you can then face outwards. Success becomes visible on the outside through our actions and achievements, even though they begin on the inside, with your beliefs and values. In 1993, Richard Bandler joked that "when we get born, our brains should come with an owner's manual". They don't, but you can create your own workshop manual for your brain, and improve the quality of your life, if you learn to manage your inner experiences. Robert Dilts has a useful model for doing just that. It shows how the inside and outside aspects of your life are related through different logical levels of consideration. His model uses these different levels to address different questions about our different working parts. Before exploring the principles take a pen and paper and work your way through Dilts' levels.

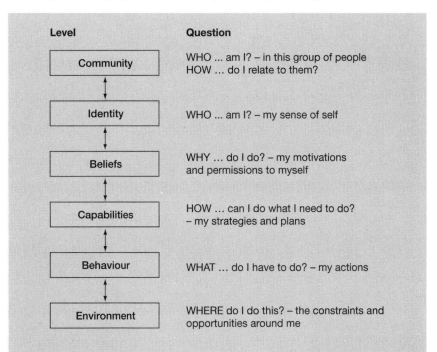

Level	Question
Community	WHO ... am I? – in this group of people HOW ... do I relate to them?
Identity	WHO ... am I? – my sense of self
Beliefs	WHY ... do I do? – my motivations and permissions to myself
Capabilities	HOW ... can I do what I need to do? – my strategies and plans
Behaviour	WHAT ... do I have to do? – my actions
Environment	WHERE do I do this? – the constraints and opportunities around me

Figure 1.1: Dilts' levels

Step 1

Inside yourself, you can start with your professional **identity**.

When you picture yourself in school and you can see yourself going about your daily work, ask yourself:

Who am I as a leader?...

What do I think as a leader?...

Thoughts are what we tell ourselves about our world. *What do I tell myself?...*

What taped messages run and re-run in your mind to constrain your success? Tell yourself something different and notice how you and your world can change, because your sense of identity shapes your values and beliefs.

Step 2

Moving down, *what do I believe about myself as a head?...*

Beliefs help us make sense of our world, who we are, our place in it and what we are able to become. We often use them to explain our past and justify the way we now behave. They often determine our future because they become so rooted in our sub-conscious, that we don't even notice how they open up or shut down opportunities for us. However, it is worth remembering that you can choose the beliefs you want to hold and so you can change them at any time. I know it's not always easy but you can change a belief by being open to new ideas, open to doubting old certainties, while noting that your belief came about in one context and that you may need to change it in new circumstances.

What you are *truly* capable of is often limited by what you believe about yourself. This, in turn, is linked to your picture of yourself. Don't you have a picture of yourself as a head? How do you think you can enhance that picture? See it in your mind's eye, right up there in front of you. Enlarge it, make it grander, brighter, full of colour. Do whatever you have to do to the picture until it feels right. What can you tell yourself about the picture? How you feel or think about yourself will shape the world around you.

Step 3

It is especially important to reconsider beliefs about your **capabilities**. They are the keys to extending what sort of head teacher you can become. The well-known saying "if you believe you can – you're right, you can; if you believe you can't – you're right, you can't" has much truth in it. Some beliefs you hold may constrain your capabilities and therefore your potential magnificence from being realised. In my experience, teachers are the most diffident class of people I know in expressing their expertise, their own genius as educators. Slow to credit themselves for their skill and quick to point out their limitations. "But I'm only a teacher" is one of the most common and most plaintive cries I hear and I live by the sea surrounded by gulls so know a plaintive cry when I hear it. Jonathan Livingston Seagull almost stuck with being 'only a seagull' but broke through his beliefs to fly like an eagle. So, have outrageous aspirations and answer the questions:

What are the outer limits of my capabilities as a leader, just now?

What is the ultimate extent of my capabilities as a leader?...

Step 4

Your capabilities govern your **behaviours**. They determine the repertoire of behaviours you have at your disposal. The more you think you are capable of, the more likely it is that you will have an appropriate behaviour to fit the circumstance. The more appropriate the behaviour, the more effective your leadership.

Is my behaviour as a head congruent with my values and principles?...

All four of these internal levels impinge on all the rest of the world out there.

As you move outside yourself, you choose appropriate behaviours for your environment. Do your actions fit with your values? Are they appropriate for this **environment**? Is the environment in which you work the best it can possibly be? Does it constrain your behaviour or extend it?

Step 5

Moving the other way from inside, you reach the higher level outside – that of the wider **community**. How do you connect with these others?

How do I benefit them?...

This last question about what contribution you make to the community in which your school sits has always been an important, but often neglected, question in a decade of intense focus on the curriculum. A result of your energy flowing where your attention is going. Your attention now needs to change. As a head teacher, your mission with respect to the community becomes more significant as the key responsibilities for more and more aspects of the school leave the Local Education Authority and devolve to you and the governing body. Even more important than this formal devolution of responsibility and accountability is the fact that effective teaching *on its own* does not necessarily make an effective school. That needs a sense of community grounded in the community.

What links all these levels are your principles which run from top to bottom, making the structure strong and true. Strengthening these at each level can become the basis of your own vertical self-development plan! You can work to integrate yourself as a head teacher with your values, with your strategies and plans for the future, with your management behaviours and processes so that they are all mutually supportive and reinforcing of your vision for the place in which you work and its wider community. As a leader, you can then influence other people's perceptions of the school at each of these levels.

The fast-food eatery at the end of the Universe: The McDonaldisation of education

In 1996, George Ritzer explored the success of the McDonald's restaurant chain which is founded on a perfectly rational business approach to feeding people. He identified the hallmarks of the fast-food restaurant as:

1. *efficiency:* this involves making a means/ends analysis to produce the desired outcome as quickly as possible. The drive for efficiency in Western society is defined by the interests of business and industry. Finding the most efficient means by which to do something is therefore considered highly rational. The three main factors which determine efficiency are *streamlining, simplification of the product* and *putting the customer to work.*

2. *calculability:* numbers are crucial to modern society – everything must be quantified. People are rounded up into groups of statistics. Success must be quantified. The allure of numbers

means that the quality of the experience can in many cases be overlooked, or even ignored.

3. *predictability:* rational people do not like ambiguity. A McDonaldised enterprise tries to ensure that surprise, disappointment and unpredictability does not occur by emphasising consistency through a well-defined operation.

4. *control:* all stages of the process must be able to be controlled, so that the predicted targets can be achieved. This calls for the constant monitoring of the process and its outcomes.

The system is geared up to achieving conformity of output through the measurement of performance and is not focused on maintaining or improving the health of the diners. I'm not saying that schooling has become fully McDonaldised... *yet...* but if you have been teaching over the last decade, you will know it is easy to find evidence that fits under each of these four hallmarks. You may look over that period and notice examples of increased demands for efficiency and better streamlining of school processes, for greater amounts of numerical data collection for calculable performance indicators, for more specific predictions of outcomes or targets, for more centralised control – in fact, a move towards a mass-produced educational experience, an eduburger.

Which way is 'up' in space?

I am sure that, when at the helm as a head teacher, you would not choose to travel all across the galaxy to end up running a fast-food eatery rather than a good restaurant; even with the present-day pressures of improved effectiveness and 'value for money'. Ritzer concluded that there is a fifth, unplanned for, characteristic of McDonaldisation. It is the consequence of the other four. He calls it 'the irrationality of rationality'. He found that each step of McDonaldisation is beguiling in the seemingly unarguable logic behind them. Mr. Spock would have thoroughly approved of each one. However, such unrelenting sensibleness seemed to always result in turning the world upside down. That is, the end result of a series of individually sensible, rational steps was often not sensible or rational at all in the overall outcomes. In a McDonald's for instance, you serve yourself, you find your own table, you clear the table – you do all the work except the cooking. It is efficient eating and has lost most of the pleasure originally associated with dining out. It is a dehumanising process. Michael Fullan has already commented on this in his research into change in schools. He asserts there is a limit to the rational approach to school improvement. However, if you don't take a totally rational approach then you have to employ an intuitive one and you are back to unconscious thinking.

As an education manager I could adopt the language of accountants and see each student as a 'unit of resource' as a university colleague once put it. I don't because as a teacher I deal with the whole person. I become involved as a whole person myself. I believe my relationship with them is the key factor in their learning. I am concerned for that person over a long and often crucial period of time for them. Nationally, are we in danger of distorting children's learning for the political security of good test results and a high position in a league table? In England and Wales there are already signs that a prescriptive curriculum and its accompanying testing regime is producing a generation of children more motivated to learn for exam results than to learn how to learn. A clear set of values is the only shield against that irrationality. Each child is hardly definable by their school uniform, their learning targets, their SATs scores or exam results or any other set of quantitative data. Equally, you as a leader are not defined merely by a set of achieved competences.

Greek mythology describes the origins of the universe in terms of order appearing out of the unorganised elements of the vast open space of Chaos. Today, chaos and chaotic phenomena have become the focus of serious scientific study. These studies have in turn provoked the development of a new discipline with new concepts and laws – Complexity Theory. This theory divides events and phenomena into four classes:

1. *Stasis* – things that have only one state of existence – they do not change
2. *Order* – those that change into a small number of possible states of existence

3. *Chaos* – those that have many possible states and are unpredictable in the longer term, like the weather
4. *Complexity* – those with such a huge number of possible different states that patterns begin to emerge which we can make sense of, but which still have little bits of unpredictability in them.

Few people would want to see schools falling into either group 1 or group 3. The question therefore is – do schools belong in group 2 or group 4? I suspect that politicians would prefer to see them in group 2. It would fit their mindsets. Because then they can plan rationally to achieve educationally and politically clear targets. Straight-line, strategic planning on a national scale is so much easier if there is not too much variation amongst schools. Many teachers would probably view schools as belonging in category 4. They are messy places. There are recognisable patterns of similarity in schools, but they all have their differences when seen close up. There is a level of natural complexity in schooling on a day to day level. In the realm of pure science, Complexity Theory says that if you try to cope by reducing the complexity to control them, systems tend to fall back to group 1 – to stasis and ossification. They fail to evolve. Many of the government-led changes of the last ten years seem to have *drained* energy from the educational system and discouraged teachers from taking part in real learning. There is a risk of the dampening down of the natural creativity of teachers in classrooms. This fits with the predictions of Complexity Theory of what happens if you try to cope with an issue by attempting to reduce its natural complexity. If pursued, the result is stasis (group 1) and then ossification – the system becomes rigid and fails to evolve. Teaching is reduced to the technical delivery of a single, tightly-defined, curriculum; teachers, merely operatives. If we train one generation of teachers to be no more than skilled technicians, we will end up with *three* generations of learners who think education is about passing tests. Without creative teachers/learners, the school as we know it is unlikely to continue as the instrument of educating our young. This could be the irrational outcome of what appears to be a rational approach to raising standards. The only way to live with increasing complexity is to let the natural creativity of the interaction between teachers and learners to flow, within an organisation that is ready to capitalize on what emerges.

Part Two

Life, the Universe
and Everything

The universal principles

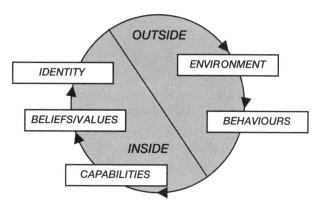

Figure 2.1: The universal levels

Don't you just know that school life is often more circular than linear? There is no up and down in space, there's just in and out and around. The Earth has a limited surface area but a traveller can wander over it forever. Einstein showed that the universe has limits too. It has boundaries. A consequence is that like the Earthbound traveller, if you continue long enough you can return to your starting point without retracing your steps. You can take the Dilts' levels and join them to form a continuous loop. Then you can decide to tour around them from any starting point.

I have started the journey of this part of the book at the inside/outside boundary, with the awareness skills. The inside recognition of the signals from outside the head. Travelling in your inner space you can move on to register your feelings about the incoming data. Then you can employ your mental skills. You can think about those responses, analyse and make decisions about them. You can then cross the boundary and move to the outside, into action, through your behavioural and linguistic ones. And here you are again at the incoming signals, the responses to your words and deeds from the community. Time to start another orbit. Current theories of uncertainty and the unpredictability of space, time and matter in modern physics have created the concept of parallel universes. It is conceivable that without Senge's fundamental shift of mind, some heads could be not just on a different planet, but in a completely different universe! The following pages contain the key principles that shape the inside head. Unlike the answer from the computer 'Deep Thought' of Douglas Adams' *The Restaurant at the End of the Universe* they do not number 42. They don't describe a moonscape but they can form a mindscape that could be your own Metanoia.

Your mindscape is built mainly from your lived experience and it shapes the principles and beliefs that govern your living. New experiences feed back into the mindscape to add to or enlarge it and so your lifelong learning is a dance between these two domains. The principles help you evaluate what to move towards and what to move away from in the world. That is, they help you choose the values that guide your behaviour. Research on leadership shows values have a special part to play in ensuring success. These studies show marked differences in the values expressed by successful head teachers and those that struggle in the role. One of the key differences between the groups of head teachers lies in the degree of clarity of their own values that successful heads bring to bear when dealing with the more messy conflicts that can arise. Less successful heads lack the guiding principles that frame the value which could help them steer a path through the maze to a happy landing. This clarity seems to be more important than which specific values are held. With clarity, these values act as benchmarks or reference points for your choice of actions in hazy problem fields.

Most definitions of values agree that they consist of criteria or standards that serve as pointers for your behaviour and that they are particularly meaningful for the individual in the selection of goals and actions. Although values encompass all aspects of thinking and feeling, they can be considered as the content of the affective or feeling domain. The content of the thinking, cognitive domain can then be thought of as the beliefs that have their origin in the values you hold. And are you clear about these? You have already answered questions related to your values in the previous section. Use them now in the next activity, to explore your values even more and more and particularly how you keep them in your mind.

Values on the line

This is one of those activities where you will know the answers to the questions, even though you don't know *how* you know the answers. Don't imagine that it's important – to know your values and preferences clearly – this is the secret of success.

1. What would be important to you about working as a head teacher? (Think of what's important to you about the job.) Write down eight things that are important to you about what you do as a head teacher. Just write down what bubbles up into your mind or what first comes into view.

    _____   ____

    _____   ____

    _____   ____

    _____   ____

    _____   ____

    _____   ____

    _____   ____

    _____   ____

2. Go back and rank them 1 to 8, with 1 being the most important to you and 8 being the least important.

3. Now rewrite them in that order of importance.

    1 _____

    2 _____

    3 _____

    4 _____

    5 _____

    6 _____

7 _____

8 _____

4. Take the most important and notice how you represent it in your mind. Do you have a picture or description of it, or a feeling about it? Or is it that you have all three? Take a minute and check the details, using the following ticklist.

   If you can picture it in your head, is it...

   ❑   bright or dark?
   ❑   coloured or black and white?
   ❑   like a photograph or a video?
   ❑   in focus or hazy?
   ❑   in a frame or more panoramic?

   If you close your eyes and you can sense it in space ...

   ❑   is it close to you or far away?
   ❑   to the left or to the right of you?
   ❑   above your head or below (or at the same level)?

5. Then repeat this for the second value and notice that some of the elements of how you represent this one are different to the first. Check out the differences – whether its image is closer or further away than the first, brighter or darker, bigger or smaller, in a different position, and so on.

6. Do this for two more and then notice how all four value images are arranged in your mindspace. Are they connected? Are they just like stars, scattered randomly or do they form constellations? Do they lie on a line – straight or curved?

I do not know what values you have chosen and cannot pretend that I know which values you should espouse. So, in the following pages, I offer you a framework of principles that you can explore for yourself.

I hold to a simple model of leadership…

At the heart of leadership lie your principles – your beliefs and the values you hold dear about your professional life. If they permeate your whole living then it is no exaggeration to consider them as truly cosmic principles. Secure in them, you can lead from that centre. You can live and breathe them. The Chinese word for life is 'ch'i' – actually it is a symbol which can take the meaning 'life force', but which is also sometimes translated as 'the cosmic breath'. I prefer this last expression, having started my professional life as an astronomer. It is also in step with the guiding metaphor of this book – headship as an exploration of the heavens. As I like to imagine a truly universal breath of life reaching into every part of that space. That breath takes shape through three overlapping sets of actions:

1. **teaching** – implies things to be learnt and someone to aid and guide that learning. Since all good teaching starts with imitation of a good model, the head's role here is in first being the leading learner and then the learning leader. One of the measures of your own skill as a teacher is the growth not just of new knowledge in staff, but the increase in their capacity to think ahead of where they are now. As the outside world focuses more and more on the teaching in the classroom, then the teaching, coaching and mentoring of the adults in the school become more and more important. And the key thing to teach others in a school and the thing to be learnt, is what reality in the school is now and just what is possible. And the second is that what is possible is always more than you think is possible.

2. **leading** – for a head teacher, this implies a place that people want to reach, a direction from where they are now to where that place is, a path to follow in that direction and someone who can find the path amidst the confusion of everyday happenings. Since the desired place is a place of learning, one of the key functions of the head is in leading the learning of the school community.

3. **mediating** – means being in the middle, rather than out in front. Heads are in the middle of the action at both the macro- and the micro-level. On the ground between national innovation and directives, and their operation in the school. In the middle, amongst their staff and community, mediating the everyday issues and conflicts of running a school. In the sense of grappling with these everyday issues, conflict *is* life. About encountering and facing up to the flow of that life. There is no change without conflict, no conflict encountered without learning to be gained. The mediator role also has the elements of moderating change, of being the social therapist, of bringing harmony to the community, through what it learns in meeting change.

The interplay between these three spheres of action is what makes the job of head teacher one of the most satisfying and, at the same time, one of the most demanding roles in society. Succeeding in all three areas is what makes it attractive. Thriving in all three is more assured when you have a well-understood set of values and beliefs. Principles to live by.

When you begin to work through the list of principles in this section, you can adopt them one at a time and notice what happens as you apply them singly to situations in school, or you can bear them all in mind and apply the appropriate one as and when it is needed. Whichever you choose, it means that you can read each of the following sections in any order.

1. Awareness Skills

Sense and non-sense!

Just what do you mean by awareness? When you stop and think what it is in terms of practical skill development, it is about paying attention, about noticing what it is important for you to notice right now. Fritz Perls believed that awareness is the only basis of knowledge and communication. This first principle reminds you that what is important for you to notice now is behaviour – your own and that of others. Leadership of a school, more than anything else, is about the communication of meaning about the school and its possibilities. Awareness of the other person is the basis of effective communication. The more comprehensive your awareness of another's internal mindscape and emotional state, the more you will be able to empathise with that person. Responding with empathy increases the likelihood of high levels of trust developing between you, followed by an increased openness to hearing what you are saying. Developing the skill of empathy in children has been an objective of the national curriculum in the last decade. Just how do you develop that skill? What are its sub-elements? The key is awareness and the rapport that comes from it. You already have natural rapport with many people. Building on that and creating even deeper rapport depends on increased levels of awareness.

So what can you consciously become aware of? The person's *external* behaviour is the most obvious. I know that you can notice patterns in:

- *body posture* – the way they hold their body – do they stand full square, or at an angle to you; do they stand straight, lean forwards, or to the side; are their hips pointing in different directions to their shoulders? When they sit with you, do they lean forward or slouch back, turn sideways or face you directly?

- *face and neck* – how does their colour change as they speak? You can notice the flow of blood into their cheeks or throat, or how the tension around the eyes changes with different topics and associated emotions.

- *gestures* – are their arms and hands still and quiet, do they move them a little or wave them about? Are the movements at shoulder level or higher, or lower? Do they often cross their arms, or legs, stroke their chin, lean on their elbows?

- *voice* – what is its pitch, volume, tempo? Is it level or highly modulated?

- *language* – do they have a tendency to use a selective vocabulary, a preference for certain words? Some people use highly visual words – they 'see' what you are getting at, get the 'picture', the future is 'bright'. Others use auditory nouns and verbs – they 'hear' what you're saying, your ideas 'ring bells' with them, things 'sound' good. Yet others use kinaesthetic words – they 'grasp' the idea, 'feel' good about it, get a 'grip' on the situation.

- *breathing* – is it rapid or slow, high in their chest or low in their abdomen? Rapid and high may indicate someone who visualises things quickly; slow and low, a more deliberate thinker, someone who has to hear himself think.

In addition you can notice some of their *internal* patterns. Through the language they use you can gain insights into their values and beliefs. Through their selective use of vocabulary (whether there is a tendency to use hearing, visual or kinaesthetic words as described above) the way they represent the world in their mind and how their mind may tackle issues.

You can choose to notice one or more of these as you listen and talk to another person. You can establish and deepen the sense of rapport between you by matching these patterns. Practise bringing your physiology in line with theirs. Subtly replicate their gestures with hand and arm movements of your own. Align your voice levels, pitch and tone. Use similar vocabulary. As you spend time listening, breathe at the same rate as them. Practise the skill of matching these characteristic behaviours one at a time. It will seem artificial and stilted at first, but like driving a car, it soon becomes natural and unconscious. You already do this to a large extent quite naturally. Breaking the skills you already have down into their separate components allows you to practise and improve

Behaviour *is the* **best** *form of information about a person*

them singly. Responding in this empathic way increases the level of harmony between you and improves the quality of your communication. Eventually you will put them all back together seamlessly to be an excellent communicator. People will want to speak to you.

Conscious awareness-skill development is about the ability to detect very fine details when necessary. Paradoxically, it is also about quietening your conscious, analytical mind because of its tendency to keep asking questions. These questions tend to get in the way of listening and watching. If you are an aware person, you can notice what your body is telling you, pick up on the small signs of muscles tensing or relaxing, of your breathing rate and depth. Body and mind are focused together on the same present moment, the same here and now. There is some evidence that a woman's brain is constructed to do this more easily than a man's. But whether a man or a woman, you can practise improving the sense of your own body and then get better at noticing these small differences in the people around you.

When I was young I thought my mother and her twin sister were magicians. They seemed to know exactly what each other was thinking, or what they were going to say next. When I was older I was told it was telepathy. That satisfied me for a while – it wasn't magic, 'just telepathy'. Later still, as a sceptical scientist, I was reminded of Richard Feynman's story of his scientific upbringing. One day out on a walk, his father pointed out a bird to him and said it was a sparrow. He then gave it half a dozen other names of what the bird was called in other countries and said "You can know the name of that bird in all the languages of the world, but when you're finished, you'll know absolutely nothing about the bird". I knew the name of the form of communication but it told me nothing about what was involved.

Now I know that my mother and her sister were just very sensitive to each other's movements, voice inflections, facial expression, etc. They could notice extremely fine differences in these and other characteristics, even though they, themselves, were unaware of just what they were doing. Although I didn't know what they were doing either, I did know that I could do the same thing with respect to them. It explained why, as a child, I could never understand how anybody could possibly confuse my mother and her sister, just because they were called identical twins. I noticed very small differences that neighbours and friends missed. However, because I didn't consciously know what I was doing, I couldn't transfer that skill and that sensitivity to other twins. I could just as easily be as confused with other sets of twins, as strangers were with my mother and her sister.

Much of our life is spent on automatic

This partly explains how some people seem to possess a 'sixth sense'. They react automatically to signals from other people that are below the threshold of their conscious awareness. Awareness skills can be improved and awareness training is aimed at changing that threshold. It is about gaining greater sensitivity to what you can see, hear and feel about your surroundings. Like Argos in mythology, seeing with a hundred eyes. Even when asleep he still 'saw' with fifty of them. With his conscious mind elsewhere, his seeing then was into his unconscious mind. As an experienced driver you know this effect really well as you have almost certainly driven a car on 'automatic', when your journey has ended with no conscious remembrance of much of the route. All the multiple perceptions needed to complete it safely were unconscious, but like Argos, you can be well aware that if necessary, the unconscious mind would kick-start your conscious mindfulness at any time. Psychologists have likened this day-dreaming state of mind to a light hypnotic trance – wide awake in terms of sensory input from the outside world, but with all your thinking process busy with internal matters. They believe we have many different trance states that we switch into when triggered by outside events. You can understand this as trance when your actions flow automatically and without any conscious thinking. It is possible to increase this way of problem-solving. And when you can extend that ability to use all your unconscious perceptions when needed of you, you too will be wonderfully intuitive – an unconscious thinker.

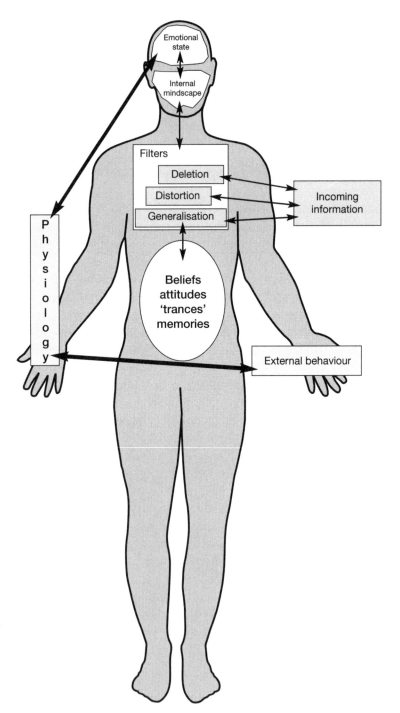

Figure 2.2: The NLP model

Scientists have estimated that the body receives about 2,000,000 sensory signals every second! From all over our body, these signals are sent from the touch nerve endings, the eyes, the ears, the nose, the tongue. Together with those producing our internal sensations, the data from all of our senses are constantly being processed and acted upon. In that processing, many people exhibit a bias towards the data from one of the senses. Some are more visual, others more auditory, both in how they accept data and in how they express it.

Whatever the preference, experiments also show that our conscious mind can cope with, on average, about only *seven* different pieces of information. We bridge this huge gap by three main mechanisms:

- we **filter** out a lot of information that we think is unimportant
- we often **distort** some of the data to match our expectations
- we tend to **generalise** what is left to fit in with our past experience or beliefs

What we filter out depends largely upon our beliefs and values and any sensory preference. They help us select the data that fits our mindscape and transfer these as chosen memories for our conscious mind, so that we can easily recall them later on. These chosen memories are often labelled with an emotion to make that recall easier. The rest of the 2,000,000 bits of data may be stored below our threshold of conscious awareness. Your *unconscious* mind notes them and may prompt you to behave accordingly. This is often seemingly irrational because it isn't conscious action. Being human, we often explain this away by describing it as intuition or by just saying "I don't know why; it just *feels* right!"

Lose your mind and come to your senses

So, often, it's our feelings that tell us what is actually 'sensible'. When we act according to those feelings we have let go of our conscious, thinking, mind and relied on a judgment about the message from our senses. This is what I consider David Leithwood means when he talks about 'unconscious thinking' and for me, it links with intuitive action. Your conscious mind can accommodate only a fraction of the total know-how and wisdom which already resides in your mind and body.

Studies have shown that when talking about how you feel, perhaps only 7% of any spoken communication is carried by the actual words! When your listener is unsure about the truth of what you are saying, your tone and other qualities of your voice will carry a message four or five times stronger than the words – some 35% of the total message. Our brains are particularly attuned to human faces and so the expression on your face and accompanying body posture will convey the strongest message of all, often overriding totally the words used. Almost all of this is below the threshold of your conscious awareness, but you can learn to hear all the nuances and the melody behind the words. The first communication skill taught in counselling training is listening – listening to the words so well that you can reflect them back to the talker, clarify them and restate them. Checking that you have heard them. This is precision listening and invaluable in a leader. As a first level of listening it is vital to understanding and is a rational, 'conscious thinking' skill. However, if most of a person's communication is in a form other than the words, then a second level of listening is required. It entails listening with your third ear – that inner hearing which is the gathering together of those many signals picked up by your increased awareness of body, movement, gesture, voice tone, timbre, pitch and volume that inform your unconsciously thinking mind. Even though this skill is more rare in leaders, the paradox is that listening intently to words at the first level is more demanding than this deeper, second-level skill of hearing the unspoken. Remember – looking, listening and touching are tasks we carry out on the surface of our being; seeing, hearing and feeling are all outcomes of the tasks that are achieved on the inside.

The intuitive leader

The emphasis on a technical approach to leadership and schools has resulted in the downgrading of the use of intuitive decision-making. Before the introduction of formal training for headship, there was a greater acceptance of the tacit knowledge of head teachers in running their schools, in their *unconscious know-how*. Straangard's (1981) model of learning progression:

| Unconscious incompetence | → | conscious incompetence | → | conscious competence | → | unconscious competence |

equates mastery of any activity with unconsciously competent behaviour in that activity. So in this new millennium, we are seeing the returning acknowledgment of unconscious information processing as a key element in leadership and teaching (Atkinson and Claxton, 2000). Recent brain research has shown that unconscious processing starts about half a second before conscious processing. There is also some evidence to suggest that the unconscious mind can make decisions about events and situations that the conscious mind cannot begin to describe or articulate. And not just decisions, but *effective* decisions. And sometimes the reasoning of the conscious mind actually gets in the way of effective decision-making. Perhaps the main disadvantage of such intuitive decision-making which has been learned in one context, just like mine of distinguishing between my mother and her sister, is that it very often does not transfer into another context. To do that, demands an additional step to the learning model above – that of *conscious unconscious competence!* Becoming consciously aware of what it is you are actually doing 'naturally', unthinkingly, instinctively (Figure 2.3). To achieve this goal you have to learn to know how you do your unthinking behaviour! Not an easy task to

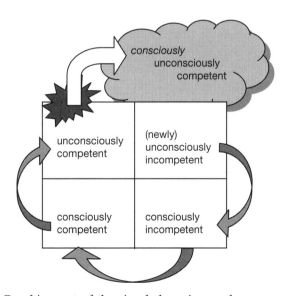

Figure 2.3: Breaking out of the simple learning cycle

undertake alone – you need a little help from your friends. All good teachers who daily demonstrate their 'practice wisdom' in the classroom, depend on highly developed intuitive reflexes, an unconscious competence, deriving out of their experience. As with all masters of an art, explanation, or even just straightforward articulation, of that intuition is difficult. You need someone who can observe you knowingly to help you describe what it is you are doing. Which is why we need to develop schools as learning to learn communities (see Part Three).

The first step when thinking on your feet is, as it says on the cover of *The Hitch Hiker's Guide to the Galaxy*, 'Don't Panic'. Thinking on your feet is about being both imaginative and creative whilst being open to new experience. New experiences are easily come by when travelling in space, as by definition, the territory being explored is new. On Earth, panic causes the blood to drain away from the cortex and limbic systems of the brain and therefore shuts down both conscious and unconscious problem solving. All that remains in a state of high anxiety are the self-preservation responses to danger of Fight, Flight or Freeze. And what you want is the fourth 'F' response – Flow – a state of focussed awareness with a deep sense of engagement in a meaningful activity. A paradoxical 'active calm' in the face of the complex task of leading a school.

Einstein once said that 'the intuitive mind is a sacred gift, the rational mind, a faithful servant'. The intuitive mind comes from the state of relaxed alertness. Different people have different ways of attaining that state. Some people use physical approaches such as particular movements from yoga or tai chi, or more meditative or self-hypnotic techniques. Others use more everyday techniques such as seeking a quiet spot, gazing out of a window, listening to a particular piece of music or doodling. What they all have in common is the stimulation of the body's relaxation response through deeper, slower breathing and the stimulation of the alpha-rhythms of the brain. This is a reduced rate of the brain's normal cyclic activity which reduces stress levels and promotes insight and clarity of thought. For me, responding to my own inner ear takes the form of the free-floating images which arise from these deeper signals into my surface awareness. You have your own way of recognising and responding to your unconscious, intuitive mind. Once you can relax in listening, this is an easy skill to acquire. So, not knowing what's going on in *their* mind, empty your own and just watch what they do and listen to how they say what they say. Shut down the consciously judging part of you and observe. Check how you feel about what you see and hear. You'll learn a lot about the other person and be able to act positively yourself. That's your choice. The rest will flow. John Heron describes this state of relaxed awareness as 'being here, now' – totally in your present situation, whilst 'being there, now' for the other person. Such relaxed awareness can also be achieved through the centring process.

Filters of the mind

This exercise is a simple introduction to what might be just some of your favourite and habitual filter options. In the following statements below, tick the answer that is closest to your preferred response in the context of leading a school. If you want to tick a second, rank order them 1 and 2.

1. *The most important thing about being a head teacher is:*
    - ❏ keeping my finger on the pulse of the school
    - ❏ maintaining good relationships with staff governors and parents
    - ❏ making sure we hit our targets

2. *The reason for becoming a head is to be able to create a school in which children...*
    - ❏ are free from the constraints of their environment to pursue their learning
    - ❏ are free to develop their potential as independent learners

3. *To keep everyone committed to our goals, I often...*
    - ❏ paint a picture of the future for them
    - ❏ explain my thinking and rationale
    - ❏ use analogies and metaphors
    - ❏ appeal to their emotions
    - ❏ encourage them to walk around and get the feel of the school

4.   *I know when I am doing a really good job, because...*
- ❏   I know inside that I've done my best
- ❏   the finished achievements prove it
- ❏   I get good feedback from my staff

5.   *In leading staff into changes, I tend to...*
- ❏   paint the big picture
- ❏   give them realistic examples of how it could be
- ❏   ensure they have sufficiently detailed and specific information

6.   *The great thing about being a head is that...*
- ❏   there is something new to tackle each day
- ❏   you can change things bit by bit
- ❏   much of the job remains the same, despite outside events

7.   *As a head leading staff in school discussions, it will always be important to...*
- ❏   stay true to my own view
- ❏   be prepared to see things from their perspective
- ❏   be able to 'helicopter' above discussions and maintain a certain distance

8.   *As a head I will be able to recognise a good teacher just by...*
- ❏   working alongside them
- ❏   seeing them in the classroom
- ❏   hearing them with children
- ❏   monitoring their plans and the children's work

Some common mental filters

The key to your preferences are:

Item 1: This indicates your prime motivator as a leader. Is it to:

1.   control what's happening (power over others)?
2.   maintain good relationships (affiliation with others)?
3.   complete the task successfully (achievement)?

The filter operating here is a *motivational driver* – it determines what is more important to you in the three main threads of school improvement – controlling the changes, maintaining relationships or achieving the goals. What is the rank order between the three?

Item 2: This filter may indicate a *motivational direction*. Is it a push or a pull? Is the primary direction of change more likely to be changing to get *away from* something undesirable or changing to move *towards* something attractive?

Item 3: This indicates a possible preferred set of language for describing your world to yourself or a preferred way of thinking.

Do you use:

1.   visual language – describing pictures?
2.   dictionary-precise language – a focus on the literal meaning?
3.   creative language – story-telling?
4.   sensations-based language?
5.   kinaesthetic or feelings language?

This *language preference filter* indicates a bias in your choice of vocabulary to one of the five groups of words. If you use mostly 'seeing' words, how well do you communicate a 'vision' of the school to someone who prefers to speak using 'feelings' words? Much miscommunication is the result of a bias in your representational system, meeting the heavy different bias in the other person.

Item 4: This is another *motivational filter*. This one indicates where the origin or the push to do something different mostly comes from – from within yourself or from without – from someone else's approval, or from the visible evidence of a completed task. (And bear in mind that perhaps 40% of your staff will have the opposite motivator to you!)

self-referenced – when you just know inside, for yourself
task achievement – when you have finished
others focus – when others acknowledge your achievement

Item 5: How expansive or controlled is your language? What scale of words do you use?
big
life-size
small, details

The *chunk size filter* indicates the level of information that you deal with most comfortably. When it comes to planning for instance, what is your preferred working level of detail? Do you prefer broad brush descriptions of the plans or much fuller descriptions?

What level of detail are you most comfortable with – large through to small?

Item 6: What is the first thing you hear yourself say as you encounter something new? Do you look to see what is familiar or do you prefer to experience the thrill of something new?

difference – first and foremost
sameness – but with some difference
sameness – what's familiar here?

This is a *decision filter* – what helps you make up your mind to do something? Is it the degree of sameness to what you know already or the degree of difference that attracts you?

Item 7: This is a *perceptual position filter*. Is your favoured stance in staff discussions that of a 'first position' perspective; i.e., direct involvement in the discussion with the strong expression of your opinions? Or do you spend more time in a second perspective position – imagining what it's like for the speaker – seeing it from their point of view or trying to grasp where they stand on the issue? Are you able to take a third, more detached position, hearing the interplay between the different speakers, noticing the relationships changing in the course of the discussion as people shift position on the issue. Moving at will between all three positions is a valuable leadership skill.

Item 8: This is a *convincer filter* – what form of evidence really persuades you of something – do you have to *see* it, *hear* it, *think* about it, or will only *doing* it work for you? And what might it mean for your management of people with a different evidence procedure?

What do these mean for you? On their own, they might mean very little. It is possible for a colour-blind person to remain ignorant of the fact for many years. They can discriminate between different colours, even though they see them only as shades of a single colour. It is often only when the two colours have the same tone or have similar intensities that they are confused. Each one of us can be thought of as mentally looking at life through tinted glasses. If we are not aware of it then we can assume that everyone else sees the colours of life as we see them. What this exercise does is raise your awareness of the sorts of filters that are common and may prompt you to identify the patterns or programmers in your behaviour. For example, if you marked 'maintaining good relationships with staff and governors and parents' in Item 1, you could ask whether you usually tend to put people before task achievement, or before the exercise of the power of your position. Or in Item 4, if you ticked the first box, do you typically put more weight on your assessment of a job, than an outsider's opinion? In Item 5, if you ticked the last box, do you find yourself more concerned about getting all the loose ends tied up right from the start and worried if you have only the broadest overview to go with?

Learn to recognize these filter patterns in yourself and then notice them in others. When you can detect them in other people you will be able to choose the words you know will pass easily through their filters so that your message is more fully understood.

2. Emotional Skills

The last section dealt with awareness of yourself and others at a visible level. Sensitivity to your own emotions as a head is vital. Emotions will signal to you the existence of any unsatisfied psychological needs you may be experiencing. For example, anger may point to a need to oppose what is happening; sadness to a need for comfort and support. Poor awareness of these needs is often why interpersonal issues may remain unresolved in schools. Such unfinished business tends to accumulate over time and re-emerge with greater depths of emotions later. We have all experienced the explosive snap of the last straw. These needs may define your values and therefore your values are rooted in the emotional or affective domain of your mind. Your values will in turn shape your beliefs and your thinking. This establishes the linkages between emotion, belief, thought and behaviour that you can be aware of.

The whole of your body is organized to prevent it from being harmed by your surroundings. It is wholly, and in its separate parts, a cybernetic or self-correcting system. If we get too hot, it takes steps to cool us down and vice versa. If in reading this book you travel too close to the sun your skin will sense damage, and produce melanin to prevent further damage. If invaded by alien bacteria, your immune procedures are set in motion. All your internal systems are harnessed together in this primary task, including your seemingly non-physical mind. This is the basic level of activity of the body. Emotions are overlaid on these activities at the next level up in the centre of the brain, the limbic system. A healthy mind in a healthy body. Although a desirable state, it presupposes that the two are different entities. Neuroscience says they are one and is finding more and more examples of how what we think in our mind affects the health of our body. If we create unpleasant pictures in our mind, talk to our inner self negatively, we stimulate negative emotions and our body responds in many ways. We can physically droop, just sag or collapse. We can stimulate a range of symptoms – from simple itching, to aches, to pains. Do this often enough and some illness or physiological complaint can follow. Neuro-linguistics reminds us that we don't 'have' a body, or 'have' an emotion or even 'have' a thought. We *are* our bodies, our emotions, our thoughts.

Knowing these connections between your mental imagery, your emotions and your physiology, you can work backwards or forwards to change emotional state. By noticing and paying attention to physical effects in your body, you can track them back and link them to the emotional state that promoted them. This can lead you to the mental image or self-talk that began the chain. You now have two powerful ways to change the middle of the chain, the emotional state. You can experiment as you read this:

Remember an incident which left you with a small niggled or slightly negative feeling.

Do you talk to yourself about it? If so, what are you saying to yourself about it?

My mind & body are one interlinked system

Or do you see it in your mind's eye? If so, what does the picture look like? Do you see yourself in the picture, is it in colour or black and white? Is it like a photograph or a video? Or do you relive it and see it as through your own eyes as it happened?

Or do you just get a feeling about it?

If so, what sensations can you notice in your body?

Once you have answered these, now...

1. *change the image in your mind – make it dimmer... or smaller... or black and white rather than full colour. Play with it and see how it decreases its effect on you.*

And

2. *if it's what you have been telling yourself... turn its volume down... or imagine it as a radio in a different room, only faintly heard...*

or...

3. *change your physiology. This is the fastest way to change how you are feeling. Breathe more slowly or deeper, or faster. Stand up, move around, look at the ceiling, shake your arms. Once again, experiment until you can notice what has the best effect for you.*

You can use this technique to experiment with mental images from other aspects of your life.

Emotions colour all our thinking and behaving

Our emotions are the feelings we hook onto our decisions about what happens to us. Also, our emotions are what often lets the brain know what it knows. We often refer to the heart as the centre of our essence, our spirit, our true self. My Celtic ancestors believed that all the power, the energy and the spirit of a human being resided in the head. That's why they decapitated their enemies and kept them on display! It ensured that the energy released was added to their own. We now know there is no one organ that can claim that unique distinction. The mind and the body are not separate entities. Modern neuroscience tells us that all the cells throughout the whole body contain the electro-chemical messengers of the thinking system that we once thought were only present in the nerve synapses. These transmitters of impulses are transmitters of the messages of our mind. One way of looking at that is that our thoughts flood throughout the whole of our body, affecting every cell. That's why an imagined fear produces the same physiological effects as a real one. Conversely, all of our body affects our thoughts. It's a two-way process. If you alter one, you alter the other. Certain bits of knowledge about the external world are stored in different parts of the body. This unconscious knowledge can influence our conscious decision-making, without us being aware of it.

An example of this is what scientists call 'blind sight'. This is where people who have 'working' eyes, but who have been rendered blind by accidental brain damage, can accurately pick up objects that they cannot see or name. The knowledge of the object is lodged in the functioning eyes and gets transferred somehow, to their motor co-ordination system, without passing through the visual cortex. They pick the object up without knowing what it is. Modern science suggests that our memory is not a place – it's a system. Not a filing system where all the memories are individually and completely stored, but a system where the basic information from all memories is spread throughout the mind. Spread in such a way that the whole memory can be reconstructed from any one part of the information system. A system that is everywhere in the body. Scientists use the hologram as an analogy for this way of storing information. Just as the flat two-dimensional surface of the hologram can produce a complete 3-D image, so the brain can recreate from just fragments of the memory data an overall picture of the original event. I know you can think of a particular scent or a piece of music which will immediately bring back a total re-living of a past experience. This is an example of the brain's limbic system in operation, stimulating the construction of very full memories.

Emotions are facts

Schools are primarily still focused on intellectual achievement. In second and third place in importance lie, probably, physical prowess and artistic talent. This may be because society rewards the demonstration of know-how and attainment in these different areas very differently. So, even in those schools in which Howard Gardner's ideas on multiple intelligences are being accommodated within the curriculum, a hierarchy of merit still seems to operate. The good thing about Gardner's idea is not that the existence of many different intelligences is necessarily true, but what is happening as a result of teachers acting 'as if' it was. They are extending their repertoire of classroom strategies and experimenting with new teaching approaches to encourage the development of different strengths. Teachers are becoming more conscious of their own preferred ways of learning, of using language that possibly favours visual learners, auditory learners or kinaesthetic learners.

All teachers can recognise the importance of personal relationships in the motivation of a pupil's learning and all teachers know the personal emotional investment they make in those relationships. It is a paradox of teaching that knowing these things we have spent so little time in developing children's understanding of emotions and the skills associated with that development. One benefit of the greater interest in teaching for different intelligences is the acceptance of the need for the nurturing of emotional intelligence. There was a time when emotions were denied and the only skill development allowed was in that of self-censorship of any emotion. Emotions have to be taken into account in our everyday life. They are real, even if self-generated, and will affect our behaviour. Although not on Gardner's original list, there is a growing awareness of the efficacy of inducting children into emotional skilful-ness. Witness 'circle time' and other approaches to behaviour management which address the emotional state of students and gives them an opportunity to complete unfinished business from the day. This psychological discharge aids the healthy development of relationships.

When you accept that emotions are facts, then you will appreciate that motivation and change are more likely to be achieved by addressing the emotions of staff as well as their intellect. Too many leaders, in denying or neglecting the emotional content of staff discussions, try to promote change through a reasoned approach alone – George Bernard Shaw's 'brute sanity'. Motivation is linked to values which arise in the emotional centre of the brain.

Emotional intelligence is more important for a head than academic intelligence

Current research shows that measures of emotional resilience are better predictors of good leaders than IQ scores. This is particularly true for head teachers. You probably know better than anyone the proportions of time you spend in your own different emotional states. You may even recognise that some are preferable to others. Do you have a favourite – one that you spend a lot of time in? Do you have a dominant emotional state – one that you particularly associate with your professional identity as a leader and which helps define who you are seen as? How much time do you spend in the different states you recognise? Knowing your own emotional profile can be a key to unlocking your resourcefulness to make changes to how you look like a head. More importantly for you is the fact that emotional intelligence is emerging as a key skill area for future managers. Daniel Goleman (1996) outlines the steps to improve your emotional intelligence as:

- know your own emotions, especially those you enjoy creating...then...
- learn to manage them... then...
- use this to motivate yourself... then...
- learn to recognise them in others... so that...you can handle relationships better.

Recognising your emotional states and becoming aware of your present state are the basis of managing your emotions. To do this, begin by noticing the important physiological differences that form part of each of your different emotions. Use the body scan questions to recognise the physiological effects of each emotion.

When you are alert, excited or anxious…

Is your pulse speeding up or slowing down? Is your breathing high in your chest or deep in your stomach? Is it rapid or slow? What are the sensations in your abdomen? Scan all your muscles. Are any contracted and tense? Is your jaw relaxed or clenched? Your shoulders hunched or thrown back? Is your whole body straight or at an angle?

These are just some of the differences linked to different emotional states that you can notice. Becoming aware of your own physiology and that of others means that you can learn to face yourself, that you can confront your own strengths and vulnerabilities. And this is the first step in developing the skill of being able to confront these things in others. Earlier I talked about adopting a centred, balanced physiology. Everyone considers that when relaxed, they stand and take up a natural stance. Mostly though we take up an habitual one – one we learned very early in life and have kept to. It is rarely a balanced one. (You can check this for yourself. Take two bathroom scales and place one foot upon each. Then closing your eyes, stand naturally. When you are comfortable, open your eyes and look down and note what each scale reads. They probably give different readings which indicate that your weight is not as evenly spread between each side of your body as you might have imagined.) Your 'natural' stance is more likely to be habitual than natural. Just as you have a habitual physiological stance, so too, do you have an emotional one. One that has certain preferences and leanings. One that may not always be balanced and centred. Moving from any disturbed emotional state into a balanced one is the last step of emotional management. Knowing this connectivity, that changes in one part of the mind-body system affects every other part, is essential to a head staying balanced.

With a balance inside, you can then move out. The outside aspect of emotional intelligence is the ability to notice the emotional balance of others. To notice it when you first engage with them and then to notice how it might shift as you speak. Caring for and nurturing the emotional health of staff has become a core management skill over the last decade of continuous change. You know how insecure many teachers have become in the face of those changes and accompanying political criticism. Carol Pearson describes an 'heroic workplace' as one in which "staff feel as secure as possible, ...find and express their genuine talents" and "feel ennobled when they are working for an organisation that is doing something positive in the world". Heroic schools "promote individual gifts and talents by holding up a magic mirror that shows them *(the children)* how they are special". Showing staff that they are special becomes a key activity for the leader. Many years after I first met the 'how do I walk' head, he reminded me that schools are about working *with* people *for* other people. He also said that he had learned that teachers are all people who have off-days and on-days, "who bring the bundle of their lives with them, though they are so often hidden under a cloak of expertise, who are vulnerable, but wishing to appear otherwise and have abilities unrecognised by themselves and by others". His job, he believed, was to help them discover and use those abilities. Not always an easy task as clouds of initiatives, local and national, descended upon the school.

3. Analytical Skills

NPQH 4(b) Decision-making skills – the ability to investigate, solve problems and make decisions.

How often do you think about your thinking? When were you taught the thinking strategies you use? Do you teach children different ways of thinking? Our natural thinking strategies are, for many of us, like our natural posture – more habitual than natural. Much of my education was based on the habitual thinking of scientific investigation methods and linear problem solving. There are other equally natural approaches that are the habits of other disciplines. Which habits you acquire in life depend very much on what your view of life is. The basis of expanding your thinking skills is the acceptance of realities other than your own, of multiple realities and that some people really do seem to come from another planet.

Mental Mapping

It's life, head, but not as you know it. A map is but a representation, a model, *not* reality itself. And the most important thing about a map is what is not on it! Obviously, for *everything* in the terrain to be on the map, then it would be as big as the country itself!

Normally, maps are just interpretations of one aspect or another of the land. So, knowing what is left *off* them is important. The second key feature of maps is that what gets *on* them is **differences** – differences in heights, rainfall, population, land use, etc. Maps are sources of information about the landscape that can shape our actions and help us decide our paths through the terrain. This is why Gregory Bateson affirms that difference is the true meaning of information – a piece of information is a difference that gives *form* to our world. That is, information is a difference that *makes a difference* to our map of the world.

Figure 2.4: Mental mapping – the map you have in your head is the result of your life experiences

We create our world by the words we use to describe what our senses tell We select from our senses what it is that interests us. What information do you select? Our own past experiences and learning help us decide what we will pay attention to in the world around us, what we will focus on. Two people can look at the same car accident and describe it in two very different ways. Two people can look at the same picture and see two different images. The word pictures we have created in our own mind to describe the picture, are just that – in our mind. They are not the original event that prompted them. You may have already explored some of the filters that shape your own mindset in the section on Awareness. You may already know that you have a dominant sensory system for accepting data from the outside world, or for expressing yourself in it. These ensure your map of the terrain is highly personalised – it has been custom-built, by you, for you to inhabit.

Objective analysis of a situation is a valuable skill. Personal or subjective analysis has often been derided. All scientists crave objective experimentation and they all know how difficult it is to achieve. They are aware that science has a long history of scientists deluding themselves, of convincing themselves of the rightness of their answer just because it was founded on flawless logic and objective, truthful, data. The best know that even when the data has been gathered as carefully as possible, so as not to be in dispute, its interpretation may be suspect because of every scientist's highly individual mindscape and perceptual filters. Interpretations have been the basis of more heated scientific arguments than disputes about the actual, original measurements. So, for me, a key skill is the ability to lay my own beliefs and values to one side, when considering those of another. When John Elliot (1991) went to investigate teaching and observe teachers in their classroom 'honestly and objectively', he acknowledged the individuality of his own map and mindset. In order to leave his beliefs and values aside, he redefined those terms as:

> *Honest – by making the personal biases and prejudices which underpin one's judgments clear to the teacher*

> *Objective – being open to critiques of one's judgments by the teacher*

This is good advice when switching into analytical mode. In the best of cases, where the school stands on a bedrock of achievement, it is possible as a leader to restrict your analysis to clarifying the goals, considering the key factors, building the strategies and taking the decisions. If you lead a school with less trustworthy foundations, then you will need to pay more attention to other building

People respond to their inner map of the world not yours!

blocks – those of principles and values and feelings. You will also need to appreciate that the attitudes you hold spring from your values. Attitudes are by origin, therefore, evaluative in their nature and can limit even our best of honest approaches to the rational analysis of a situation.

One common example of how worlds differ is that many head teachers rate themselves more highly as managers and leaders than their staffs do – that's *their* world, *their* reality. It's obviously not the world of their staff. To gain the trust of staff, you will first have to explore *their* planet. You have to meet them there, understand its ecology, become familiar with its contours and its rocks. You will also need to speak their language. Being amongst staff and mediating mindscapes. This is the way to gain rapport and is the basis for motivating them to explore other planets themselves.

Strategic thinking

Analysing things strategically in school starts from the results of the enquiries you (the community of learners) have already made about:

- your beliefs and values
- your dream of the future school
- the purposes it will serve

Having checked where you are now with regard to currently held beliefs and intended purposes, and with the dream in mind, strategic thinking marks out the journey step from here and now to there and then. This is straight-line thinking:

1. create and set the vision
2. communicate the vision
3. build commitment to the vision
4. organise people so that what they do is aligned to the vision and this leads the mind to thinking logically that there is a fifth step…

HEAVEN!

This makes strategic planning seem deceptively simple. Deceptive because such planning presupposes that the future is largely predictable. However, even if the landfall is mapped, no sailor and certainly no astronaut points their craft exactly at the proposed landing site at the moment of launch. Both know that there are invisible if not unknown forces at work between launch and landfall, whether they are tides or gravitational forces, and so start slightly *off* course. Hitting the desired landing point then demands a constant appraisal of the path covered and decisions on the possible alternative ways of traversing the remaining distance. So a good course plan contains within it plans for moving *off*-course. Perpetual steering! It's a complex, intuitive, and for an experienced navigator, unconscious thinking exercise. The secret of future successful headship is likely to be the skill of recognizing what is emerging from the complex conditions of the journey and then making the necessary adjustments.

Systemic thinking – the circles of the mind

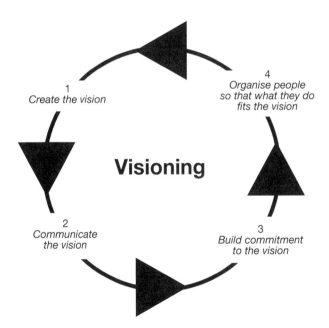

Figure 2.5: Systemic thinking – the circles of the mind

Now you know that straight-line thinking is far too rational for a school, then you may need to start with a piece of circular thinking. (A would-be astronaut really needs to understand some physics to go space travelling.) My own early training in analytical thinking was very linear. All the approaches seemed to follow the straight-line pattern;

$$Start \longrightarrow step\ 1 \longrightarrow step\ 2 \longrightarrow step\ 3\ etc. \longrightarrow End$$

with goal or target achieved. Life isn't that simple, is it? If it is simple at all, it seems to be simple circles, or at least loops. Nothing in the universe travels in straight lines. Planets and stars go in circles on circles on circles, and even these wobble as they go. The linear approach to problem solving above seems analytical and logical. However as the atomic physicist Niels Bohr once complained to a colleague, "You're being logical, you're not thinking". So we are wiser to bend the straight-line approach around into a circle as we did with the Dilts' levels. More than that, quantum physics, which followed on where Bohr left off, informs us that the whole universe is like our integrated mind/body – just one large interconnected system. It's a bit like an air-filled 'bouncy castle'. If one person jumps up and down on its surface, everyone else wobbles. School communities are like that too – what one member does, ripples out to affect everyone else.

A key feature of systems is that any movement causes not just ripples, but eddies. These are small circular movements that feed back into the main disturbance. Some will be clockwise, some counter-clockwise; some will help the original movement, some will work against it. Researchers have noticed this effect happening in human systems, in schools even!

Developing a shared vision and getting the team to work towards it are the third and fourth of Peter Senge's disciplines. The fifth and last is systemic thinking. This is a way of thinking about, and a language for, describing and understanding the forces and inter-relationships that shape the behaviour of systems. It helps you see how to change organisations more effectively and to act in tune with the larger world processes. In this example of developing a shared vision, you must think systemically. If the vision is the thing you *want*, systems thinking can tell you what you have *got* and what is happening to its growth. There is a tension between these two states. It is a dynamic approach to problem solving just like the 'off-course' steering of boats or spacecraft. A dynamic systems perspective helps you think in terms of continuously developing agendas and issues. So strategy emerges – and the key to working to an emerging strategy is the process by which your school builds and deals with an agenda of such issues.

Think of some of the eddies that could emerge as this movement begins to reach into the school.

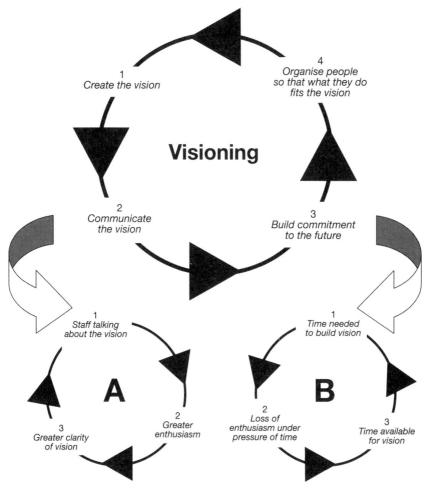

Figure 2.6

You could think up other circles to attach to the central visioning one, all of which will either add to or subtract from the direction of the original energy in the system. Shadowing a head teacher even for a few days, you can soon feel how disjointed a typical day is. And how different each 'typical' day can be! You can watch her move through a wide range of tasks in a very short time. You can listen as he deals with a parent, a teacher, a young child, a teacher, an inspector, a builder and hear the changes in vocabulary, in voice tone, in psychology, in emotion. You can admire the intellectual and social gymnastics involved in all these reactions to the different eddies from that one central circular movement. It is easy for a head teacher to drown in the eddies. Circular thinking prepares you to better anticipate the future, to recognise and to accept any-time delays brought about by contrary circles. It also allows for unlooked-for swirls. All this keeps the central circle in perspective and its timescales realistic.

Language limitations on thinking

Finally, how do you limit your thinking skills unnecessarily? It is possible to deny yourself the full use of all your brain capacity by the imposition of your beliefs and values on your mental faculties. Values have been described as the thoughts we tell ourselves about how our mental maps ought to be. How many of your thoughts are really (th)oughts? Notice that word 'ought'. Bigger than UGH and smaller than nought. And for me it means some-thing between those two words. What does it mean for you? Does it constrain your thinking and your analysis? Does it blind you to possible solutions?

Human beings appear to be born with a built-in programme, an instinct, to help them acquire language. Steven Pinker labelled this 'mentalese' in 1994. He believes that our genetic make-up prepares us for language development. It seems to be one of our survival systems because our brain rapidly absorbs the complexities of our first language. It gets progressively slower the later in life other languages are learned. According to neuroscientists, if we want to really develop foreign linguists, we should start the second lan-guage programmes for children between the ages of 3 and 10. After that, mentalese and the neural pathways that we could have used to learn language seem to become less effective, leaving us with basically the pathways of the language(s) we have learned. So the language system we acquire may set some of the pathways for our thinking.

A different native language, produces a different set of neural pathways in the brain and a different mindset – a different map. Just remember Mr. Spock and his attempts to make sense of the emotional language of the humans on the bridge of Enterprise. His brain was wired differently to theirs!

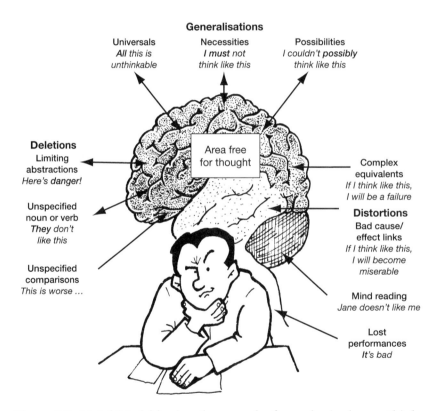

Figure 2.7: Metal Model brain – how much of your brain do you think with?

You can get clues to those parts of the brain you are not using fully by listening to your language. The picture shows you a selection of commonly used words, expressions and sentence formations that indicate a no-go area of thinking. This classification is known as the Meta-model of language. Look at the different sets. Do any sound familiar to you? Are any specific ones used frequently in your school? Do you know someone who uses one or other of these linguistic patterns regularly?

> *Listen to yourself saying your most frequently used one and notice how you feel. For example, just feel the difference in your own motivational levels between 'I have to do it' and 'I should do it' and between 'I need to do it' and 'I want to do it'. Sense what sort of barrier to further thought some of these are for you. You may find by just seeing and hearing them so plainly that you can now get past any internal language barrier and move into the thinking space that is beyond it, but not explored yet.*

When you have explored some of your own off-limits areas, you will be surprised how easily you can hear them in the speech of others. Grappling with them to achieve clean communication between you and the other person is well worth the effort. Changing the forms of speech you use will create new neurological pathways in your brain. New pathways may mean you can become a different thinker! The activity at the end of the section on communication gives you some examples of these forms of speech and ways of responding to them to improve your own communication.

The universal S.A.T.

This is not a universal Standard Assessment Test, though it could be, as you will apply your numeracy and graphicacy skills to your use of language! Alternatively you could think of it as a universal Situation Analysis Test. A health check for the suitability of your plans. Remember the Chinese curse – 'May all your wishes come true'? Some of the things we think we want, do not, in the end, bring the benefits we desire. I use this exercise to really explore the likely future outcomes of a course of action or of achieving a target and check that what I desire will really benefit me.

Step 1. Take a target or course of action and add it to this stem:

I want to get (or do) X

X being such things as 'I want to start a breakfast club', 'I want to introduce an appraisal system for learning support assistants', etc.

Step 2. Take a sheet of paper and place the question in the positive quadrant of a Cartesian grid.

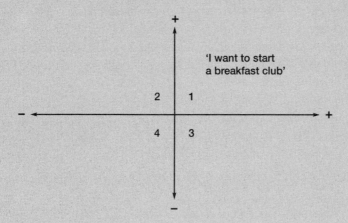

And then apply the standard + and - mathematical rules to the sentence to produce its inverse, its converse and its non-mirror image reverse(!).

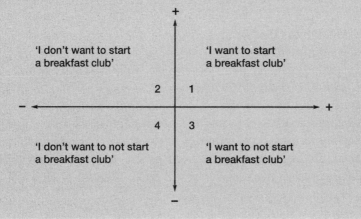

Say these in sequence and feel the difference between them. What does each one say to you? They are very different aren't they? The real test comes by following this process with this next set of questions about the action X. Brainstorm as many answers to each of the quadrants taken in the order shown.

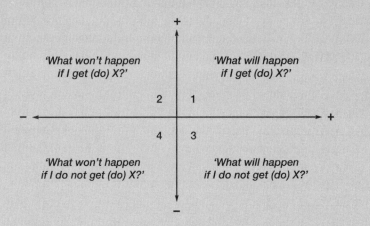

When you finish, look at all your responses and then decide whether the action or target is what you really want to happen.

4. Linguistic Skills

Communication

NPQH 4(c) Communication skills – the ability to make points clearly and understand the views of others.

Good communication is the key to effective leadership. From the last section you will understand why I think this NPQH statement is back to front – good communication is receiver-based first and sender-formulated second. To be able to make points clearly, you first need to understand the views of others – you need first to be familiar with their map. In that case, listening is the first step – gathering information, noticing the linguistic patterns and the true message being sent. Listening with the Meta-model of language in

You cannot not communicate

mind ensures that you can notice the gaps and through the gaps perceive the mindscape. You may then be able to talk effectively. And by effectively I mean more than just getting your message understood – I mean talking to bring about change. Engaging in dialogue is the key. Peter Senge differentiates between dialogue and discussion. For him, discussion is a conversation aimed at arriving at a decision for action; dialogue is a conversation designed to get at or to develop mutual meaning and understanding. Effective talking bridges the gap and changes dialogue into discussion and then into action. I have found these definitions useful in leading staff meetings. The clear difference in the intended outcome of talk that is defined as dialogue rather than discussion, makes both more efficient and effective. People are more willing to offer an opinion when they know no decision rests upon it and that the desired outcome is increased meaning for all.

Have I reached the person to whom I am speaking?

Merely standing still and silent conveys a message to another person. You may think you are communicating nothing, but the other person will read messages into that silence and that stance. When you speak, your choice of words will add to, clarify or distort the original message. *How* you say the words will be more powerfully interpreted as their tone and tempo will produce an emotional reaction in the listener. Have you experienced an exchange with an angry parent, who afterwards accused you of being very rude, when you thought you were especially calm and controlled? Someone who didn't hear the actual words but read something else into your actions? When you move, the number of other signals sent increases dramatically. Do your actions suit your words? Or do they say something different? Different messages from different parts of you can confuse. Worse, such mixed messages can prompt distrust. And remember, messages 'leak' out from movements we might not even know we are making.

The **meaning** *of any* **communication** *is the* **response you get back**

Misterious messages

Winnie the Pooh was often confused by 'messages'. It's not surprising, when they were of the sort *"gon scerching. bisy bacson"*. Many communicators are too busy talking to notice the effect of their message. For my purposes a missage of mine is a communication where I assume that the recipient of my missage must know and understand its meaning just because *I* have thought and said it. The surest way to know what you have 'said' to another person is to listen to the response you get back. You may know what you intended to convey, but if the response does not confirm that your particular message was received, then you know you didn't convey it – you sent a missage. You will have to repeat it as a message – something they can understand. You will probably have to say it differently. The words may stay the same, but perhaps your tone of voice or your posture will need to change. You may have to say it in many different ways to finally get a response that lets you know the message has arrived!

An episode of *Star Trek* had the Voyager team meet up with the aliens known as the Children of Tama. Communication was difficult because whilst both groups used the same vocabulary, they had different meanings in the two cultures. It wasn't quite as bad as the Mad Hatter in *Alice in Wonderland,* who had words mean whatever he wanted them to mean. The Children of Tama used words metaphorically and they always related their metaphors to past experience. The Voyager crew first had to realise this and then undergo a common experience to be the basis of their first true communication. Most school leaders face this latter task of finding a common experience to aid understanding at some time in their career.

Being aware of the continuous flow of feedback, spoken and unspoken, is essential for effective communication. For as long as you acknowledge that the responses are giving you vital information about the other person's understanding AND you are able to remain flexible in *your* responses to that feedback, you are successfully communicating! Many difficult appraisal interviews can be traced to this lack of attention to the appraisee's responses to your feedback. And this notwithstanding the fact that you thought you were being 'fair' and evenly balanced in your appraisal.

'Difficult' people are those you give up on when you, in turn, cease to be flexible in your responses to them and communication is broken off. Resistance is not so much an attribute of *them* but more a measure of *your* inflexibility of response.

Beyond the sound barrier – the Meta-model of language

In the previous section, I drew your attention to the limited use of the brain that is indicated by what people say. The language categories in Figure 2.7 were first identified by Richard Bandler and John Grinder. They called this classification the Meta-model of language. You can use the Meta-model introduced earlier to improve your communication skills and restructure your thinking. These figures of speech indicate that the speaker holds certain assumptions or beliefs that limit their thinking and therefore their behaviour. Getting below the surface of the language pattern to uncover the assumptions can liberate the person from the belief and increase their resourcefulness.

> You can discover the abilities that are hidden behind the belief. In this exercise, choose a language category from the left-hand side of the table that you know you use, and write out what you say. Then ask yourself the question from the right-hand side of the table and notice your response. Do this for as many of the others as you like. That way you can become tuned into these figures of speech in others and be able to choose an appropriate response which will get closer to the meaning of the communication.

Language pattern	Clarification strategy
Deletions	
Simple deletions	*Recover the missing information*
I am angry	About what? about whom?
They don't care	Who, specifically, doesn't care?
She's a better teacher	Better than whom? better at what, compared to what?
Unspecified verbs	*Recover the behaviour*
He annoys me	How, specifically, does he annoy you?
Nominalisations	*Change the noun back into a verb*
Communication is bad here	Who's not communicating what to whom?

There are
            no resistant colleagues
   just
     inflexible
   communicators

Generalisations	
Universals	*Challenge the generalisation*
I always miss out	Always?
I could never do that	Never? What would happen if you did?
Possibilities	*Challenge the impossibility*
I can't possibly do that	What stops you? What would happen if you did?
Necessities	*Challenge the necessity*
I have to do that	What would happen if you didn't?
Distortions	
Mind reading	*Find the fantasy*
She doesn't like me	How do you know?
… because …	How does that mean she doesn't like you?
Lost performances	*Find the actor*
It's not right to …	Who says it's not right?
	According to whom?
	How do you know it's not right?
Poor cause-effect links	*Find the actions*
You make me angry	How specifically?
	How does what I'm doing cause you
	to become angry?
False equivalences	*Challenge the link*
She's a poor teacher,	How does her leaving promptly mean she's not
she always leaves	a good teacher?
on the dot	Don't you ever leave promptly?
Presuppositions	*Uncover unspoken assumptions*
If she knew how busy	How do you know she doesn't know?
I am, she wouldn't	What is she doing?
do that	What are you choosing to do, to be so busy?

Speaking with Martians

Think of someone whose behaviour seems alien to you. Behaviour you would feel incapable of. Someone doing something you could never see yourself doing, saying things you could never bring yourself to say. How do they do that? Their seemingly incomprehensible behaviour springs from the beliefs and values that they hold. The value sets that people live by can make them seem as though they come from a different planet. Clare Graves categorised ways of behaving or thinking in terms of sets of values that people hold on to. He first divided behaviours into two parallel universes – one in which individuals put themselves first and the other in which they put the greater good of the larger group above that of their own personal needs. Within each of the universes he imagined different world views which shaped the behaviour of the people on them. I have given his worlds names to fit this book:

The SELF universe	The OTHERS universe
1. Planet Survival Values are meaningless. You just need to ensure you can keep warm, eat, drink, sleep.	2. Compatria The world is mysterious. We must stick together for safety with our own people.
3. Egomania This world is tough and hard. Only the strong survive so be prepared to fight for what you want.	4. Conformarama There is only one right way to achieve stability and order – obey the rules of the system. We can all be guided by a higher authority.
5. Planet Competition We have the technology – we can overcome the deficiencies of the physical world and achieve our heart's desires – if we are careful.	6. Planet Co-operation We can form caring communities in which everyone can share the fruits of the planet and grow and reach their full potential.
7. Existentia Humanity is in danger of collapse – we must restore it to health by learning to stand alone and being true to ourselves.	8. Gaia There is only one world, we must work together to nurture it or we will destroy it and ourselves with it.

Currently much of our society behaves like the population of the fourth Planet (the value system that underpins world movements like the major religions or secular ones like communism). The armed forces may be immigrants from Planet 3. In much of the western world many large businesses are on Planet 5 – the value system of capitalism. Recently we have seen the emergence of the Planet 1 people, sleeping rough on city streets. Most caring professions including teaching seem to come from the Planet 6 value system.

Clare Graves stressed that these are ways of thinking about the problems we face, not types of people. No one planet is better than another. We can inhabit any one at appropriate times in our life.

We can belong to more than one at the same time. We may act as if we are from Planet Co-operation in our professional life and Conformarama in our family life. However, each planetary population finds the thinking from at least one other planet really hard to cope with. Planet 4 thinkers usually find individuals from Planet 7 particularly difficult; Planet 6's have problems with those from Planet 3; and Planet 5's with Planet 2.

In schools we often see these differences more clearly in what staff do or say to each other. Here are some examples of what the stereotypes from some of the planets might say on two different aspects of teaching:

	Doing the job	Professional growth
Planet 3: *Egomania*	I don't care about change, provided they let me get on in my classroom.	I could do better if they would just give me more time, space, money.
Planet 4: *Conformarama*	Provided they tell me what to do I'll be able to do a good job.	I'm sure the head knows what's best for me; that's what they're paid for.
Planet 5: *Competition*	I know what's wanted here and I can get the results.	If I can do a good job now, I'm sure to get promotion.
Planet 6: *Co-operation*	A school is a team effort and we all have to work together for the good of the children.	Different pay and promotion prospects can be divisive as we all contribute to the children's success.
Planet 7: *Existentia*	Are we really teaching children to be ready to fulfil their potential in the next millennium?	I want a career that allows me the chance to grow and which gives me a challenge.

Such language indicates the value base of the person speaking. Because values are the motivational drivers of us all, uncovering and understanding the value planet of another person is essential if you are to communicate with them to improve their commitment to the school's goals. The Meta-model enables you to clarify even further the beliefs and values of staff and so help in choosing language and vocabulary appropriate to each value stance. I suspect that you will need to manage people in different ways because they are on different planets to you. In your own school, would you say the governors and/or the head teacher are operating pre-dominantly out of value systems 4 or 5 or 6? And the staff? Most schools have staff scattered across the whole solar system; or at least, from Planet 3 to Planet 7 or even out to 8! Talking to them all in a language they understand simultaneously would be so much easier if Douglas Adams' babelfish which could translate what was said to you in any language while stuck in your ear was a reality, rather than a fiction! Is there a system which best exemplifies your school? And which value system does the government normally speak from with respect to schools? And is that appropriate?

5. Behavioural Skills

NPQH 4(d) Self-management – the ability to plan time effectively and to organise oneself well.

Behaviour

Self-management is a lot more than planning time effectively. For me, organising oneself well means much more than being systematic, well-informed and efficient. It means my ability to manage my emotional and intellectual states and through that, my behaviour. This demands skill at moving between the levels of Figure 1.1 and congruence between identity, beliefs and behaviours.

Who speaks first is neurotic!

I never minded being neurotic about the good of the school and have always been willing to take the first step to attain the greater goal. I am sure that when you take any initiative in your school, you do so out of that best of motives – the ultimate good of the students.

Take a deep, slow breath.

So does everyone else.

Take another breath.

Every
behaviour *has a*
positive intention
at some level

Every
behaviour is
useful
in some context

It may not always seem that way to you, but somewhere, at some level, everyone behaves out of a good intention. It may be hard to see it from your viewpoint. You will have to see it from theirs, to get a feel for what it means to them. But, whatever it seems like to you, their behaviour is intended to be useful to them or to be protective of their well-being. They may not be able to tell you the positive answer, even if you knew what question to ask. By using the questions of the Meta-model, you may get clues to what their intentions are. Harvey Jackins (1965) says "every single human being at every moment of the past – if the entire situation is taken into account – has always done the very best he or she could do, and so deserves neither blame nor reproach from anyone including self. *This is particularly true of you.*"

You know that the children in your school are innately full of joy and happiness at heart. When they come to you they may have those aspects hidden by layers of negative qualities from past unpleasant experiences or the unhappiness of their current lives. You already use the logical levels of Figure 1.1 intuitively. As a teacher you take care to describe the child's *behaviours* as not acceptable, not the child as a person. You nurture the growing child. You promote the emerging identity, whilst modifying their behaviour. You know that what they do is not who they are. You also know that within the bounds of the formal education system, much of your work is at the level of capabilities. Extending those capabilities so as to give those children a wider choice of behaviours. So with staff.

In reacting to the behaviour of others that we find challenging, we are faced with choices. On the spot. We delve into ourselves and, with the best will in the world, respond. We do the best we know how. Would you *honestly* do anything less? Your response is the best you know how to in the circumstances, because the terrain of your map may just obscure alternatives. If you cannot see them just now, then your choice of action is limited. Holding these principles in mind helps centre us in responding to behaviours that seem to obstruct rather than promote common goals. The behaviours may seem to do nothing but obstruct from your viewpoint, but be assured they will have a utility, a positive effect, somewhere, for someone in the system.

People
are not
their behaviour

Your
current behaviour
is the
best choice of action available
to you just now

Management

NPQH 4(e) "Head teachers draw upon the attributes possessed and dis-played by all successful teachers in the context of their leadership and management roles…"

You can make a difference!

It is possible to identify which of your behaviours are geared to maintaining systems and structures in the school and which are aimed at stimulating, promoting and sustaining changes. Some people use this classification to distinguish between management of a school, and leading it. Do you think it would be useful to you to be aware that solving the immediate problem – getting today's tasks done, supporting the staff in their classrooms today – are classified as management? And that taking the longer-term view – working to change the culture, developing people and relation-ships – as leadership? If so, then you can ask yourself what amount of time you spend on either group and is the distribution of your energy between the two groups appropriate for you, given where your school is on its journey, right now. You can apply the same questions to your own personal path. Can you honestly say that the balance between maintenance and change is right? And what do you need to change in your life to achieve your goal? Do you have the flexibility to change whatever behaviours are neces-sary?

We are all capable of making changes in our own lives. Living these principles is one way to do this because you have potential you are not yet aware of and you do not know yet how they will be expressed. Changing your mind demands flexibility as well as an openness to believe something new, or, at least, to doubt that your present way of working in the relationship will ever change anything. Only the insane expect to change things by continuing to do the same thing over and over again! It might have worked for spinning a web, but Robert the Bruce's spider wasn't dealing with human beings. The more you can live these principles which make changes in your leadership behaviour, the more successful changes you are able to make.

The head teacher
with the greatest degree of

flexible behaviour
is the one most likely to
get the responses
and changes needed

or

If what you are doing
isn't working
do something
different!

Discussion about the responsibilities of headship always have a heavy feel to them, conjuring up images of the noble head bowed under the ever-increasing weight of these responsibilities. I prefer to talk about a head teacher's response-abilities. To have good head teachers who are able to respond appropriately to the events around them. Heads that stretch and spring back into their natural shape under a stressful force. The scientist's definition of plastic is where the substance remains distorted after being pressed out of shape. Have you ever placed your lips gently over a broad elastic band and then quickly, but carefully stretched and unstretched it? If you do so, you will experience a startling change of temperature. The force exerted upon the band to stretch it gets converted into heat energy as it unstretches. Absorbing the energy from outside you and taking it into yourself, and then being able to release it when appropriate, is a valuable ability for heads to acquire! Acquiring it might just stretch you! It starts with the centring described earlier, with grounding your whole being in your key principles. You can become an elastic rather than a plastic head.

Stretching is one of the most noticeable effects of taking up a new sport. How often have you cried, "I've discovered muscles I never knew I had" after taking up some new form of exercise? The muscles have been there all the time – you just hadn't noticed them before. Their use and presence in your body had been beneath your awareness. In the same way, we have many latent intellectual and emotional strengths and abilities that often do not surface until called upon. Trust yourself. You can exercise those change muscles – try a little something new each day and amaze yourself with increasing suppleness.

Developing your flexibility, your response-ability, requires practice in stretching and pulling. It can take time to change your behaviour subtly. Start by just making a small difference – do something much the same as you always do, but just change one aspect of it. Drive to work, but keep strictly to the speed limit! Brush your teeth with the opposite hand. If you need to, work up to greater things. Like most people you can discard an old habit and replace it with a new behaviour in about a month, if you remember to practise it daily. New behaviour can be learned by

You *have all the resources you need to change your own behaviour*

small actions. Large change can be achieved, like the completion of a long journey, by the repetition of small actions, of single steps. (Twenty-three repetitions and it becomes a habit!)

It helps to change successfully if …

you can first get a feel of what the new you would be like.

For instance, go inward and ask yourself…

"What would I look like if I was leading a successful school?" Then create a picture of yourself on the ceiling, as if you already behaved like that. See yourself up there, leading successfully.

Remember your role model and recall times when you have already led successfully.

Now stand up and bring that picture in front of you and step into it…

…look down at your feet and experience what it feels like to be that successful.

In the last section you explored the misterious message and the principle of the 'meaning of your communication is the response you get'. You can apply this to your management behaviours. What if you held the principle 'the meaning of your management, is the results you get'? This would mean that if you didn't get the planned results in terms of continuing improvements in teaching and learning, you will need to change your management activities. You will have to do something different to what you are currently doing.

You can manage your staff by managing yourself. A school is first and foremost a network of relationships. The quality of a school is determined by the quality of the relationships within it. Bad relationships are the result of things both people involved have done in the past, and building a good relationship is a lot easier than struggling with a bad one. It does mean, though, that you have to begin to change your side of the relationship. Because you exist in a relational network any change at your end of the linkages is bound to alter the other ends and the people attached to them. That is, you can behave differently – by changing your mind about what you do. I won't pretend that you can do this easier than you think. However, success in your mission will come as you know how to stretch your ability to learn and change. You can become more responsive without losing sight of your vision or your mission.

Leadership

NPQH 4(a) Leadership skills – the ability to lead and manage people to work towards common goals.

Redrawing the map

Leadership is often the art of changing the maps of reality in people's heads, not reality itself. John Harvey-Jones once described the prime task in his leadership as "holding a mirror up to the organisation". The skill he was promoting was that of being able to create in the minds of the staff a picture of the school. What it's like now, what it's currently doing – a common image that gives them a common language to talk about it, so that everyone concerned gets a sense of what is happening. Only then can they attach a meaning to their tasks and actions and harness them to the development of the school.

Earlier, I talked about how two people can have totally different maps in their head, even when they both stand in the same landscape. Most often, it is not the incident or event that takes place that is the problem, but the person's response to it. The reason is that they are seeing it from a somewhat different position from within their mindscape. Seeing from different positions has a startling effect on your thinking. Many people picture development planning like a stairway to heaven. If you see things this way what you look at are the risers in the stairway, the things to get above and past, and the energy needed to move upwards. What if you picture the action plan from the position of its achievement? Now you see all the goals that you have accomplished rather than the obstacles to be overcome. Just changing the picture in your head

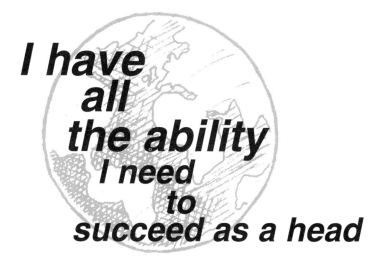

I have
all
the ability
I need
to
succeed as a head

will change your mental map and therefore the way you think about the problem.

Take a current goal of yours and look at the upward-going stairway and notice how it feels to see all the actions you need to take to achieve it, as you describe in your head the achievement of the goal, using the future tense.

Now stand up and shake off that image.

Look at the stairway in the second picture with yourself at the top of the stairs. Now think of the achievement of the goal as if it is now accomplished. Then describe it to yourself using the present tense.

Notice how you feel and notice the difference between that feeling and the one you had with the first image.

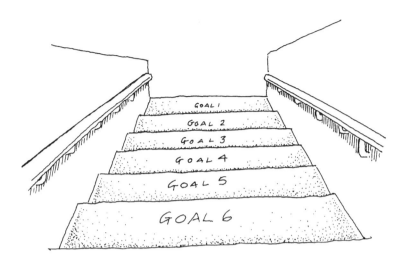

You can do this verbally also. Imagine you can reframe conflict as discovery. Just notice for yourself what happens. Discovery means, does it not, that there is something new to be learned. If you learn something new each time, then there is no failure.

Someone can say something offensive to you. Whether you are offended by it is a choice you make. You can take offence or you can refuse to take it. A simple technique to develop this skill is to ask yourself, 'what can I learn here?' If you find yourself in conflict with a colleague, then instead of sticking with your point of view, find another viewpoint. It doesn't have to be theirs, it can be from some point on the terrain where you can see where *both* of you are standing. That way you will find it easier to move them to another position and in so doing, change their viewpoint and therefore their point of view. Doing it skilfully is an art to be mastered.

Alien views

Some leaders seem to get their message across, effortlessly. How do they do it? What is the set of skills they use? One of them is the ability to see a situation from a number of different points of view, to put themselves into different positions. Specifically, they can not only stand in their own shoes – a 'first' position – seeing the situation from their own viewpoint, they can also move to a second position – that of the person they are talking to and feel what it is like to be them. Even more, they can rise above it all to a third position, that of a neutral observer, and hear both sides of the conversation. At this higher level, you can detect patterns, and whilst noticing gaps in any particular pattern, you can know what is needed to complete it satisfactorily. First class communicators move between these positions easily. You, too, can do it once you do this exercise.

Think of an example of a recent conflict or of an unfinished exchange with someone else. Standing, or sitting where you are, (call it position A) mentally mark out three other spots in the room, B for you, C for the other person having the exchange, and then D for an observer.

Firstly, in position A, where you now are, look at B and C and notice what you see, hear and feel. How are they relating to one another?

Now move to your place B. Notice your behaviour in the exchange from your point of view – what were you seeing, hearing and feeling through your own senses? What was important to you in the exchange? What was not being dealt with?

Clear your mind, shake off being you and now step over to the other person's place C. Imagine yourself as the other person. Look at it from his/her viewpoint. What was important there for them? What was not being dealt with?

Once again, shake off the other person and move to position D. From here you can see positions B and C of the exchange and your original spot A, where you began thinking about this issue. What do you notice in the interactions between B and C? What resources or supports are needed there? What can you notice that you didn't notice before? What might need to change? What advice can you now give the person in A about what you could bring to that situation, now that you can see the whole picture?

Take the answers to all these questions back to your original spot A, and check that you feel better about the situation. Notice how your perceptions have changed. Consider how you will behave towards the person next time you see them. What you will be able to say differently?

Reframing experience like this opens up your mindscape and helps you recognise a resource you possess, but have been blind to. Recognising this in yourself, you can help others take up different perceptual positions. You can help them to recognise a behaviour from one context and then transfer it to a new one; to realise they have a capability that has not yet been exercised; that a belief that was true and helpful in a different place and time is not necessarily true or helpful in the present; that they are different now.

One of your development goals as a leader can be to become more skilled in the process of reframing experience for another person… for constructing models and theories which help to explain some things that that person's experience has led them to believe may be true about their own mindscape… helping them discover what they already know… for leading their learning. For being a teacher. And the best way of becoming skilful in reframing is to apply the process to yourself until you can believe now that you have all the ability to succeed. So that, like Carl Rogers, you can say to yourself "I am enough, for the situations I face".

Part Three

What is headship today?

Take me to your leader!

What do you *expect* out of being a head teacher? Do you admire the **symbolism** of the role – the fact that everyone can identify the role? Or do you wish for its **autonomy** – the freedom it gives you to make your personal mark? Do you feel pride in the command of the *variety* of skills you will need to exercise in the job, if you are to be successful? Are you excited by its potential *impact* on so many people and the future of the community? Or is it the fact that the job well done has so much immediate *feedback* from staff, parents and children? To begin answering the question in the title, let me offer you a paraphrase of Carl Rogers' words (1983):

Headship in the first place is a process, a direction, not some static achievement.

So, headship over the next ten years for those of you engaging in it is a process of being and becoming the head teacher that only you can be. Does that fit with your expectations? At the beginning of this book I asked you to picture a good role model for your own headship. Was it their achievements you valued or their way of being? What did you want to emulate? What would someone on your staff want to copy about you? What would you want them to learn from you? When you have answered that last question, you have discovered a little of your own individual genius. And you have begun to answer the next.

How do you know you have headship in you?

This is an adaptation of a question of Peter Senge's. His question was about leadership generally, so his own answer to his question remains appropriate to my rewording of it. "You can feel the spirit of people who are excited about creating something." Creativity is not some wonderful attribute accorded to the very few. It is a skill that can be learned and developed. Moving to a school-wide state of exciting creativity follows a clear path with an established sequence. It begins with a strong, clear and desirable vision of the future school. This is followed by a period of successful problem-solving, resulting in an increasing capacity for everyone to learn and act on that learning. The final act is the appropriate extension of power to all those that have to act, to be self-directing within the guiding vision. These define broad boundaries of the headship universe – the creation and articulation of shared aspirations for the school (the leader towards the fore); the active problem solver and manager (the leader in the middle of things); the empowering of others (the leader from behind). Headship is the journey through these galaxies.

Putting it all together – working the principles

If, in leading a team, you don't remember my fourth principle *'everyone lives in their map of reality*, not reality itself, and think that others have the same mental map with regard to education and schooling, then communication amongst the members of your school, will only be partial. Transformational leaders are those who aim to bring about changes in the culture and shape of the organization in terms of its members' beliefs and feelings. As team leader, the onus is on you to understand the maps of others to better bring about these changes. Just stop for a few minutes and check out what you know, or believe about the abstract concept 'change'.

Take a pen and some paper and check your presuppositions about change by completing the following sentences:

1. *Change is ...*
2. *For me, change has been ...*
3. *I think change should be ...*
4. *If only change wasn't so ...*

Look at what you have written and ask yourself what assumptions lie behind these beliefs. Taken together, how do they define your reality? Are they likely to be true for all your staff?

Could you believe something different?

Ask yourself "why do I believe that?"...

Ask it again of the answer you just gave...

And ask it again of the second response...

How can you, as leader, avoid organisational problems that are the result of the perceptual differences between the many different realities of all your staff?

This is difficult because, every member of your staff is a potential change agent. For me change has always been too important to leave to the lone leader – wearing a head teacher's wings does not bring with it automatic and exclusive rights to omniscience. However, either as an 'emerging' leader or as a newly-appointed one, your strength lies in your personal mind map with its focus on excellence. Such a mindset is the ultimate protection against the ebb and flow of government initiatives, parental pressure and public opinions. My lasting impression of visiting a range of quite different schools in Cape Town was that of the clarity of the vision and purpose in each school. The leaders and their staff knew what they wished to achieve for their learners, regardless of outside influences, legislation and even the government. They had the courage of their own educational convictions, saw themselves as the best informed change agents and were not afraid to stand up for their beliefs against government-introduced curriculum reform, as long as it was in the best interests of the learners as they saw them.

One of Michael Fullan's (1999) change principles is *'You cannot mandate what matters'* – the more complex the change, the less you can force it into existence, because change is non-linear, its outcomes often uncertain and sometimes perverse (remember the anticlockwise eddies of Figure 2.6). One way is to follow Fullan's advice that you should first *articulate* publicly what you value; then seek to *extend* what you value by embracing the different values of others. This way shared visions grow out of personal visions. This is how they derive their energy and how they foster *commitment* – and commitment is what you want – not *compliance*. Because they are personal, your own vision will have been generated from your own, highly individualistic map of the world and will therefore include 'blind spots'. Group sharing of values and visions, or whole group 'visioning' helps illuminate the personal blind spots of each member of the group. This sharing process, (shown in Figure 2.5) had the four steps of:

* co-creating the vision

- communicating the vision
- building commitment to it, and
- organising the people to achieve it

as one way of reinvigorating a school's zest for learning.

To prepare for the first two steps, write your personal vision statement for a number of different audiences:

1. Your staff
2. Your students
3. The parents of the students

Each time use a wide, multi-sensory approach with a vocabulary that is appropriate for each audience – i.e., use a mix of sensory (VAK) descriptors to create maps in people's minds.

You can repeat this for a range of issues about the school because language programmes the unconscious and the unconscious mind will direct your energies to achieving that vision.

However, I warned you of the superficial simplicity of such linear thinking and drew your attention to the sorts of eddies that accompany any change process. To minimise the retrograde eddies you can:

1. Acknowledge the currently perceived group reality of the school by engaging in dialogues which identify personal maps and blind spots in them. Explore the hierarchies of beliefs and attitudes amongst the staff and the dominant thinking styles and mental strategies amongst the main opinion-formers.

2. Influence people to view reality at the different levels of the Dilts diagram, remembering the fifth principle - *People do not respond to reality itself but to their map of reality*. Your leadership task is to change these maps, not the perceived reality.

3. Develop a creative, motivating tension based on the pull between the group vision and the current reality.

The learning school

Much has been written about learning communities. Although there are many examples of schools that are learning communities, there are few 'how to' guidelines that guarantee its achievement. It's easy to see some of the things that get in the way of a learning community of peer professionals:

- the physical structure of schools into separate classrooms;
- the hierarchical power structure;
- the relentless improvement initiatives of regional and national politicians;
- the promotion of competition between schools through comparisons of pupil achievement and public exam; and
- competitive awards for value-added education or the 'most improved school' in the country etc.

As a head teacher it is worth remembering that *teachers* are the real knowledge engineers of the knowledge-creating school. One of the tasks of schools today is to explore how information technology can be used to accelerate the mutual learning of its teachers to benefit the learning of its pupils. However, the new technologies of information communication do not really hold knowledge – they only hold information. The information flows through them to be made sense of and become knowledge in the learner. Which means that it is the head teacher's task to create an environment that allows these knowledge workers to learn firstly from their own experience, secondly from the experience of each other and thirdly, from the experience of the children that they are teaching. That is, to create a system for sharing the knowledge of its teachers, in which they learn to function as members of the school community in which the knowledge is situated. They then have to synthesize their tacit knowledge of the learning of their pupils with that of the school leadership. They develop their professional skill by working collaboratively, by supporting each other to reflect on and make sense of, their singular experiences in their classrooms and their shared experience of working in that particular school.

Learning levels

I like to keep things relatively simple, so knowing that my conscious mind can usually only hold five or six bits of information at any one time I try to confine myself to theories that have only half that number of ideas to keep hold of. A useful one for considering change in schools is one used by cybernetic scientists - the concept of a 'black box' or a 3-step model to describe how a system functions, which we could apply to a school. The box is 'black' – because we cannot usually see clearly what goes on inside it. (Governments may see schools more like black holes in space in as much as they suck in lots of energy!)

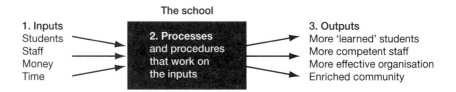

The issue for all organisations, not just schools, is, how do they survive in a world in which the inputs change year on year and expectations of what the outputs are, also changes. The usual methods are to tinker with the inputs where possible and more frequently, to change what happens *inside* the box. We have seen externally imposed changes to many of the processes – the curriculum structure and content; teaching methods and approaches to learning; staff roles (lead teachers, advanced skills teachers, consultant head teachers, etc) and training; management systems (performance management and appraisal, pay and reward systems, etc.). They are all come about as a result of a comparison between the actual outputs and the desired ones – the school's (or national) strategic targets. This is the familiar process of strategic planning:

Step 1: where are we now (sensing the environment)
Step 2: comparing the answers with where we want to be, and then
Step 3: initiating appropriate action – deciding what do we have to do to get there

In 1973 Gregory Bateson called this response of an organisation in adapting to its changing environment, Level I Learning. This is also called *single-loop learning*. Most learning in schools as organisations seems to take place at this level. Bateson went on to describe how learning can take place at different logical levels.

To move up to his Level II Learning, the school would need to take time and stand outside its box to look at what it was doing at that Step 2 and question its own assumptions. It would need a Step 2A. Examining assumptions and beliefs which might be limiting its repertoire of behaviours at that point. Looking at its own flexibility to do something different. (Principle no. 13 doesn't just apply to head teachers – it applies to the whole organisation.) This is *double-loop learning*. If it can do this, the school has begun to learn how to learn! You can see how this corresponds to the Dilts levels in Figure 1.1 (p. 23). The school has moved up a level to explore its capabilities. You can also see that Level III, IV, V and VI Learnings are also possible.

Being in the right orbit

Leading the learning of the staff members of a school can occur at each of the Dilts levels. It involves making connections between the experiences of staff at the different levels; their actions, their beliefs, and their 'identities' (their roles within the school organisation). As the school leader, you can choose to operate at one or more of these levels - it's important however, to know just which level you are currently operating at! And your role at each level is slightly different – each role shift demands a different set of skills. Robert Dilts (2003) has labelled the role at each level to give an indication of the main functions being carried out by the head teacher at each level.

LEVEL	Key question	Activity	Head teacher role [After Dilts (2003)]
Community	HOW How do we as a school enrich the wider community?	Clarifying, asserting what we are here for, why we exist	*Awakener*: renewing the sense of purpose and mission of the school in its community
Identity	WHO Who are we as a school team?	Creating the team spirit to achieve the goals	*Sponsor*: acknowledging and supporting the growth of the person as a person
Beliefs	WHY Can we identify our purposes and goals?	Developing common values and meaning	*Mentor*: helping clarify the staff's beliefs and values
Capabilities	HOW Strategic planning	Using and developing everyone's strengths	*Teacher*: extending the mental map and thus the capabilities of the staff
Behaviours	WHAT What do we have to do?	Clarifying what is needed from everyone	*Coach*: giving feedback that helps the team perform at their best
Environment	WHERE/WHEN External opportunities and constraints	Describing/defining the operations to achieve the task	*Care-taker*: ensuring surroundings that are conducive to learning

There are at least four conditions for the development of a Level II Learning community:

1. It must have sufficient flexibility and diversity (the law of requisite variety) to match the increasing complexity of our times (Principle 13 – *the school with the greatest degree of flexibility is the one most likely to get the changes needed*)

2. It must have *spare capacity* (usually achieved by creating some form of redundancy in its present activities through greater overlap of goals – no organisation can learn from its activities by engaging in a Step 2A if performing in Steps 1,2, and 3 takes all its time and energy. How can you put Principle 13A into practice – *if what you are doing isn't working, do something*

different – if you don't create space to consider what the different activity should be?

3. Minimum critical targets – keep it simple. The larger the number of clearly defined objectives you have, the more difficult it is to find the capacity to do condition 1 and the more you constrain the flexibility demanded in condition 1 above.

4. Create the conditions for double (or treble, quadruple and even quintuple!) -loop learning.

Is this a pipe-dream? It is interesting to pick out from reading the many accounts of successful head teachers at work in their schools, just what they were doing at each level. Doing the right thing and choosing the key levels at which to intervene, mostly intuitively and sometimes very consciously. And knowing at which levels they themselves were most competent and ensuring that other key colleagues could operate skilfully at the levels that came least easily to themselves. If the primary task of the school leader is to be the lead learner in a learning community, then the core purpose of an educational authority or school board is to support them in that learning. And that would take a Level II learning education authority or learning school board – an even more complex enterprise and therefore possibly rare and alien beings on this planet – although there have been reported sightings! As for a national government, subject to the pressures of the short-term-ism of regular re-election, its chances of reaching Level II Learning is infinitesimally small. Which makes it more important for schools to operate on a foundation of core values and beliefs, which can stand against Level I interventions by a government, even more necessary. So look out for some barriers to double-loop learning in your school. Does it have:

1. a fragmented organisational structure – one that works against the sharing of knowledge?

2. an over-accountability for performance, where on-the-job performance becomes an end in itself rather than the means to the end of student learning?

3. a gap between what you say you will all do and what you actually do? Is there a gap between your espoused theory and your theory in action? Remember my first Principle - *behaviour is the best information.*

Then if they exist, work out how to drop those barriers or break through them. Gareth Morgan (1986) points out the danger that the conflict between the requirements of learning and self-organisation on the one hand, and the realities of power and control on the other can promote an identity crisis in the school!

Adult learning

We know enough already about the underpinnings of good adult learning to be able, theoretically, to create the physical and psychological conditions for a learning school:

- choices in what is to be learned – self-directedness;
- learning style matched with any teaching style;
- appropriate sequencing of any new material, to step them from what they know towards what they don't know; out of their comfort zone into the unknown
- frequent feedback and acknowledgement
- support, combined with a challenge that is matched to the degree of learning robustness of the individual.

An organisation that has all of the above, operating in a positive learning climate; one in which learning builds on the staff members' current knowledge and experience, where leaders value each one as an individual and help them relate new learning to their future day-to-day work. In any work place, the connection between work, learning, and innovation is utility: teacher learning is only meaningful when it impacts (sooner or later) in the classroom.

What does it really mean for the head teacher to lead in a community of supported, self-directed learners? It means first and foremost, a reappraisal of what it has meant traditionally to 'lead' such a community. McClelland (1961) identified three primary motivating drivers behind human action, three basic needs that humans seem to want met. He labelled them:

- Power
- Achievement
- Affiliation

Barriers to satisfactorily meeting these needs are threatening to our self-esteem. Such threats, generate three corresponding social anxieties in times of change or in new situations, such as taking on a new headship:

1. the need for power results in a **performance and control anxiety** – the desire to be competent and achieve; to excel at what we do and be responsible for our own actions; to direct, guide or influence others. Our behaviour is designed as if to answer such questions as: *Will I be able to do what I have to do? Will I be up to it? Will I be able to manage the situation that I meet in that school? Will I be able to take the school forward?*

2. the desire to achieve promotes a **personal goal and orientation anxiety**. The need to make a significant contribution; to be noticed, acknowledged – a visible presence. Giving rise to such questions as: *Will I understand what's going on? Will I be able to make sense of it? Will they understand me and what I would like to see happen? Will I be able to make things happen – to change things?*

3. Wanting satisfying human relationships generates an **acceptance and inclusion anxiety** about the desire to be liked – to be trusted and to have authentic relationships with others (see Rogers, 1983). So the internal questions are: *Will I be liked? Will I like them? Will I be accepted? Will we be a harmonious, effective team?*

For new head teachers, the desire to satisfactorily accomplish change is often their highest, initial driver. So, reading this book as a potential leader, you may be more likely to be motivated to learn when you want to achieve something, hoping to transform the school you are appointed to lead. You will bear in mind that learning is an anxiety-producing activity since learning presupposes that you are voyaging into uncharted skies, into areas of ignorance.

Of leaving your home planet, your comfort zone and moving through your own personal Zone of Proximal Development towards new galaxies. You will be mindful that all learning paths bring some initial confusion, uncertainty, frustration, and sometimes, disappointment. All of which are threats to your self-esteem. Which will surface the above anxieties – and anxiety distorts behaviour. So be aware! Can you recognise your own uppermost anxiety? Given these social anxieties, it is not surprising that sometimes, learning can be something to be avoided; why so many people seek simple answers to complex questions and why many of us give up certain learning paths. Even the second human to walk on the moon, Buzz Aldrin admitted several years after the successful Apollo 11 mission that, "if we'd known then what we know now, we'd never have gone"! From Apollo 11 onwards, each landing was a huge learning experience for the individual astronauts and the mission crew as a team. But what if Mission Control in Houston hadn't itself been a learning organisation? Apollo 13 may never have returned. However, leading and maintaining a school as a learning organisation is not an easy task. One of the charges laid against NASA long after Apollo 13, with the Challenger disaster, was that it had ceased to be a learning organisation. Two decades later it had even forgotten that charge and sadly, with the second shuttle disaster, found itself accused of not learning from its past mistakes, once more. All would-be transformational heads have to be prepared to be a model of learning about their own learning – to be double-loop learners, lifelong.

One of the drawbacks of an externally imposed quality assurance system such as the British government watchdog (the Office for Standards in Education – OFSTED), is that it identifies failure. Indeed, in Britain, at its start, the OFSTED organisation took the identification of failure as its primary task. Unfortunately, teachers like many other professionals, have a high level of success, rarely experience public failure and therefore are not accustomed to learn how to learn from failure – they stay as Level I learners. The opportunities for double-loop learning are small. Historically, teachers worked for long time in a world of common situations (in a loose federation of personal classrooms – what someone once called 'professional balkanisation') and, except for the first year of their career, mostly unobserved technical expertise. Such physical isolation works against the development of shared good practice

So when the single-loop learning strategy of most teachers goes wrong, they usually become defensive, unaccepting of criticism and begin to blame others or the system. They shut down their learning just when they need it most. They sometimes collapse to Bateson's Level Zero Learning, just reacting to the criticism by devising social defences to cope with their felt anxieties. So OFSTED's focus on failure ensured that they found failure, by sending teachers crashing out of their stable orbits into a downward self-critical, self-driven spiral of incompetence. The teachers' behaviour was adversely criticised; which diminished their beliefs in themselves, which limited their capability, which further decreased their behaviour. Which eventually damaged their sense of identity. Learning about oneself is threatening and resisted if it looks like it is going to change your self-image too radically! All change opens up this risk to self-image. Particularly if the change is viewed detrimentally from the start. With its teachers categorised as unsatisfactory, a school very rapidly became classified as having 'serious weaknesses' and in need of 'special measures'. One consequence for many schools was that some of the staff were driven into early retirement or even worse, ill health. OFSTED saw this as just getting rid of incompetent teachers. In their map of the world, these teachers were probably the reason why the school was failing in the first place! And yet, there were many examples of this being the 'reality' of the inspectors – and not necessarily the reality for other observers. I have a head teacher friend whose proudest boast is not that he led a school categorised as failing, into becoming a centre of excellence, but that he did it "with the same staff" – those self-same staff classed in the first assessment by inspectors as failing teachers, but seen by him as people whose anxiety betrayed their true potential. Little wonder that on receipt of a national leadership award, he could claim with no false modesty "this is not about my work but recognition of the whole staff". What it meant for him was that he had to work successfully at all the higher levels of the Dilts diagram to restore the staff's pride in its identity as a group of people, capable of, and committed to, making a significant difference to the community by enhancing the life chances of their students. He held on to Principles 14 and 15. *You have all the resources you need to change* and *you have all the ability you need to succeed.* And by believing them himself, changed the mental maps of the staff so that they held the principles to be also true for themselves.

Schools have a good track record of turning novices – NQTs - into expert teachers, because we hold the principles to be true for them. But with the rate of change in educational practice getting faster we need to get good at turning expert teachers back into novices. What I mean by that is, we have to get teachers to carry on being willing to learn all through their career. However, teachers generally have a desire for stability and so change is risky and its consequences unpredictable. Which means they often stick to what works for them. Some successful schools have got into difficulties by carrying on doing that which made them successful. They have become locked into a vision that was relevant three or five years before and have failed to notice that environmental changes have made the vision redundant. They have limited their future, by sticking with what they were good at in the past. More fundamentally, remember that values are a funny, personal mix of thoughts and feelings and are liable to conflict at times in our life. Professionally, we must be prepared to continually assess our values against our life experiences. This is equally true of you as leader! One of the downsides of the vision-creating process above is that the brightness of some visions can blind us to opportunities for enlarging the vision. So, at some point, a critical question for you as leader may be:

How can you shape and reshape *the vision, given the complexity of change?*

For this, you have to operate at the higher levels of the Dilts diagram. As an established head, it may be that you will have to forget the original linear strategic planning process and let the new vision emerge from action rather than preceding it. As you do, you will need to stay aware of the assumptions you make through your own perceiving processes with all their deletions, distortions and generalisations. All humans have an ever active survival instinct - a driving desire for safety, or at least a wish to avoid harm. This instinct is essential to our living and is shaped by our beliefs and values, but when you are a leader, it sometimes works against the development of a learning school. The physical self-preservation drive translates socially into anxieties about one's self-esteem in the face of colleagues. And, remember, anxieties distort behaviour. This can generate some anti-matter – or at least some 'false' principles which oppose and cancel out the key principles advocated in Part Two. Some examples of such limiting beliefs held by some leaders are:

1. **A good leader is in control** (of herself and the school) at all times. This is put first because many people who seek leadership positions are motivated to do so by McClelland's Power or Performance and Control need.

2. **Negative emotions are an indicator of loss of control** and therefore to be avoided. For those people with a Performance and Control anxiety, anger is often the strongest negative emotion – and everyone equates an outburst of anger with a loss of control.

3. **A good leader always comes out on top in any confrontation** (if push comes to shove, it has to be a 'Win' for me even if it means a 'Lose' for you).

4. **A good leader is always rational.** After all, rationality is a sign of high-order thinking skills, of a highly educated brain. A commonly deployed back-up strategy to support anti-principle no.1 above, is to wear the opposition down with relentless sanity. However, remember Fullan's (1999) warning "rationally constructed reform changes do not work", because it is *irrationality* that shapes the social operation of most human organisations.

Recognise them and beware!

The head as learning leader

One of the key skills of headship is in the creation of a personal vision for the school for which you are responsible. I have already mentioned a second skill, that of negotiation. It is not enough to have a personal vision. It is certainly not the essence of school leadership to impose that vision on others. This second skill is about discovering the visions of others and negotiating a common vision for all. You lead not just one school, but as many schools as there are people in it. Each member of the school has a different image of it. Each image has its own validity for the person holding it. Your task is to manage this diversity, to help a single image emerge from the many different ones. It is similar to that of the teacher of a sculpture class. Assisting each member of the group to arrive at an individually satisfying representation of the model from the many handfuls of clay. You can motivate people externally by someone else's attractive vision, but the highest levels of motivation come when they are moved, internally, to achieve goals in their own vision.

Even your own two eyes give your brain two different images of the school. If, like most people, you have a dominant eye, its image will be the one that your mind will deal with; the other will be over-ridden. (You can check which is your dominant eye by holding a pen up at arm's length and aligning it with an object on the far wall. Close one eye, then the other. The eye for which the object stays in line with your pen, is your dominant eye. Remember that since the image from the right eye goes to the left half of the brain and vice-versa, this test is an indicator also of the dominant half of your own brain.)

The strength of a vision is that it governs and shapes the actions you take to realise it – to make that mental image real in the organisation. Gareth Morgan coined a word in 1986 to describe this process – 'imaginisation' – making the word, flesh. It is the actions and results that flow from this image that makes visioning so important. If as a Martian you had to work backwards and deduce the guiding image and aims of your present school only from the daily actions in the school and its results and outcomes for its pupils, what would it look like? Doing this exercise can be discomfiting, because if the conclusions you come to are not the outcomes you want, then these are the true meaning of your management and leadership. And one of your tasks will be to help everyone accept what currently is and to show them what can be. And then to create a tension between the two like the stretched elastic band. A tension that will bring energy to bear on achieving the desired future state.

Children's attainment is a direct outcome of the quality of teaching they experience. The main management challenge facing new head teachers is ensuring the continuing improvement of the teaching going on in the school. For me this means that everyone engaged in teaching must be engaged in their own learning, must be a professional learner. Your task then becomes the development of a community of learners.

The key question for you is whether you want to develop a learning community in which everyone looks forward to the learning they can each create for themselves and others. A commitment and a hunger for learning that no amount of external regulation can dampen. A school of gourmets, rather than fast-food eaters, where learning is savoured, rather than gulped down. The challenge comes in encouraging a learning climate – one in which all members of staff can trust enough to experiment in their learning and engage colleagues in the process, to get them to talk about their teaching in terms of:

- this is what I've done differently
- this is what happened and what it means for me
- question me on it and add to (or subtract from) it
- what do you think it might mean for you? (and us?)

and where this sense of continuing curiosity and mutual learning is shared with the children. This trust starts with respect for every other person's planet of origin and for their professional mindscape. It is sustained by adhering to the principle that everyone is well intentioned when engaging in this learning process.

This is a way of thinking that presupposes that what you know about teaching is peculiar to you and your classroom experience so far. It is an acknowledgment that what you do works for you, but questions whether it works for anyone else, including your students. Is it a personal myth or a wider truth? Is it in your mindscape alone or do others see the same view? Are you willing to be interrogated on your teaching mindscape and be open to changing what it means for you? The culture of the learning school is based on this willingness to first enquire about your own professional practice and then to share your tried and tested techniques with your colleagues. If, as a teacher or as a manager, you are always researching your own experience, you will need a robust theory of your own ignorance and a high level of emotional resilience. You have to 'walk the talk' – to have a lifelong commitment to your own learning and development; to be congruent in your words and action; to be the learning model for others. My belief is that if teachers have these presuppositions for learning, then the children will follow their example. It is a process that a head teacher needs to firstly model in their own professional practice and then nurture in others. All the while, realising that, like landscaping a garden, bringing it to maturity requires time and patience.

The head as leading learner

You can create a peer-learning culture in your school for its children and its staff to improve the quality of teaching and learning. But when you address the questions in the last section to your own headship, where is your peer-learner group? Who will ask those questions of you? What management practice myths do you maintain? Who will challenge and support your headship mindscape? If, as it is claimed, most head teachers do their best work in the period between their third and seventh year in the post, what happens after that time? How will you ensure you remain a learner in leadership? A common approach is the use of a 'critical friend' to both challenge and support your headship. Sometimes a colleague head teacher fills the role. Sometimes a manager from another domain can better ask the naïve, Man from Mars questions that prompt a radical shift in your mindscape. Another strategy is that of the action learning set – a small group of head teachers who work with each other on a regular basis, on each other's leadership and management issues. Whatever strategy you use, everyone agrees that every head teacher needs to be a lifelong learner and to have a little grit in their oyster to produce a real pearl of a school.

The dancing school

Learning can be thought of as involving all our understandings gathered together in some cognitive map in our head and the mindscape of our in-the-world experiences which make that map meaningful. The act of learning then becomes a two-step dance between the cognitive map and the experience map. New experiences bring new understandings; new cognitive insights prompt us to experiment with new experiences. It is not always a smooth painless dance. When we gain a new understanding we move from what was a comfortable state of unconscious incompetence (ignorance was bliss) to a discomforting realisation of our lack of skill or knowledge – we are now consciously incompetent. This is the first shock wave of a new headship – the realisation that promotion to this post has rendered you newly incompetent. Motivation can dip at this point as fear of the unknown rises. Maintaining motivation through this period is not always easy. Which is why the reassurance of a mentor is so invaluable in helping you continue through this transition to the pleasure of conscious competence and then on to unconscious competence. If teachers are to be always learning, they will necessarily travel through this cycle periodically. You have to ensure that the environment and culture of the school supports the fluctuations in confidence in the different parts of the cycle.

When demands on the school are so variable and so frequent as they are at the start of this second millennium, everyone needs to keep learning to remain competent in their work. Working the learning muscles is both energising and also tiring. Teaching is both emotionally and intellectually draining work. Supporting staff in maintaining a healthy work/life balance is recognised as one of the factors in staff motivation and effectiveness. I don't really like that term as it implies that work is something different to life – it isn't: it is (or should be!) a subset of life. Leading staff away from the inverse – the danger of life becoming a subset of work – is a key responsibility of all head teachers – and one that some not only forget, but actually draw their staff into, because they model that unhealthy state themselves– for them, their job *is* their life – that's their universe. You can avoid that mindset, by remembering and living your principal values. Perhaps like doctors, head teachers should take an educational version of the Hippocratic Oath – 'First, do no harm'. Your knowledge of the maxims of NLP will prompt you to rephrase this positively – perhaps as 'Do only good'.

Learning with a purpo(i)se

Learning is the central activity for all schools. Gregory Bateson (1973) tells the tale of porpoises he once watched being trained. A porpoise was taken into a training pool. As it swam, the porpoise was given a fish each time a desired manoeuvre was observed. The porpoise soon learned to repeat this chosen manoeuvre. It was simple stimulus-response learning. After rewarding this behaviour for some time, the trainer stopped and returned the porpoise to its rest pool. The next day, the porpoise immediately began to repeat the previously rewarded manoeuvre. The trainer ignored this but rewarded a newly noticed action. The porpoise soon learned to repeat this new behaviour to get its fish. The process of rewarding only a new manoeuvre continued for some days. One day the porpoise became increasingly more agitated during its rest period. It couldn't wait to get into the training pool. When it did get in there, it went through an amazing sequence of many new and different manoeuvres with no bidding. It had moved to the higher level of learning mentioned earlier. It had moved from the content curriculum to the process one – it had learnt to learn in that context.

We are mistaken if we believe that the curriculum of the school is just that defined by a nationally prescribed curriculum. That people do believe this is shown in how some people want to prescribe how many hours and minutes of each day is spent on any one subject area. Worse still is the attempt to prescribe how any particular hour of learning should be defined down to the number of minutes. A one-size-fits-all curriculum. Yes, there must be a content curriculum. Yes, hopefully it will be centred on subject-matter that is appropriate to learners who will still be working in the year 2050. But the key curriculum for today is the higher level one – the process curriculum, the one that is about learning to learn. The danger in making the first, any national curriculum, so tightly defined is that it may well get in the way of the second. It is this second which will be more important for today's students, not the other. Although seemingly rational, making the school curriculum more centrally controlled, more predictable in its delivery and outcomes, making the outcomes more tightly quantified, may be the ultimate irrationality, if its consequence is the lack of flexibility through the failure to learn-to-learn by today's children. Ritzer's worst fears would be proven prophetic.

There are times when central direction in terms of a national curriculum, literacy hour, numeracy hour, homework times, etc. may make you feel as if in a prison or an iron cage. The process above could help teachers turn it into a rubber cage. It may even produce an escape tunnel into a training pool where staff and students, like the porpoise, will want to be.

I believe that teaching can learn to be an evidence-based, (re)searching, profession. An effective learning organisation is one that supports and encourages my learning to learn, within a team context. The head teacher's role of enhancing team learning presupposes the recognition of the school's needs in the frame of a shared awareness of constraints and opportunities. For this specific group of people, this school, this bounded world, data generated by the dialogue process above and the dance between experience and understanding is real evidence – provisional and local, but still evidence. This is because it has a pedagogical meaning and a worth ascribed to it by the practitioners who have uncovered it. It becomes *valued* – and valuing information is the key to the utilisation of any data. The disregard of this valuing dimension may be the prime reason why currently most educational research is ignored. It does not matter how rational the research, how erudite the analysis and how persuasive *rationally* the conclusions, if practitioners have no *emotional* attachment to them, they will not be converted into practice. Just think of the gulf between the rationale and the practice of giving up smoking for most people.

What's the difference that makes all the difference to a school?

The answer is people. Can you become in*form*ation as defined earlier, for the people around you? That is, do you believe that you can be the difference that makes the difference? Do you aspire to help others to increase their capacity to grow, to be successful?

Your own continuing development as a human being depends on how you relate to your colleagues and in that sense you can monitor your actions on an ecological basis. Don't you think you should monitor and evaluate the physical and psychological health of the school you lead? With the growth of target-setting in teaching and learning, could you develop and publish performance indicators for these two dimensions of the school? Would such measures as incidence of smiling, rates of illness and absence, laughing levels, have a place in your school improvement plan? Do you lead ethically? Do your decisions enlarge the self-respect and self-image of your colleagues, or diminish it? Does your behaviour develop personal integrity in your relationships and professional courage in your staff? Does what you do open up or close down the capabilities of others?

The distribution of leadership and power underpins the relationships. Uneven power bases can distort them. If power stays at the top, it can flow only one way. A head teacher has to travel the spectrum between giving absolute direction to the school community (making unilateral and sometimes lonely decisions, determining the how, where and when of some courses of action) through to giving the power and leadership away (eliciting ideas from staff and going with them, giving way to the superior pedagogical knowledge of others). Research shows that inexperienced heads make many more unilateral decisions than collaborative ones, whilst successful heads give more decision-making powers away as they become more expert. This is especially so in tackling messy problems where the problem space is cloudy and obscure. The expert head-as-problem-resolver knows that answers that are more right, more ecological and healthy, for the school and its whole community, are likely to emerge from the collective mind of a group of learner colleagues than from a single brain.

One leadership analogy I liked earlier in my career is that of the orchestra. Its conductor has to ensure that every instrument plays its own notes at the right time in the right sequence to produce the overall flow of sound that the audience can appreciate. The conductor has limited powers to 'ensure' this happens. It will happen only with the consent of each player. The score is obviously the National Curriculum. Lately, I think a better musical metaphor is that of the jazz band. A team of virtuosos creating beautiful sounds around a looser theme. Orchestra or jazz band, at the end of the piece, the applause is for whose performance? You can have your own appropriate metaphor – a dancing school, a plant, a voyage – the choice is yours.

Once you become a successful head, the biggest personal challenge for you in that future is likely to be in letting the warrior role go – letting go of the need to demonstrate your own performance and achievement and giving your controlling powers away, appropriately. Then, learning to engage with all the others that work directly on the improvement of the school may become your core activity, not controlling them. Because control is not necessarily the best strategy for success in an ever-changing world. All head teachers know this, which is why research also shows that even inexperienced heads are more collaborative than the average manager in other industries. Another reason is that, as the how-do-I-walk head wrote, many years later into his headship, "for some of us there comes a day – a very painful day – when we begin to glimpse that many of the blocks in our institutions are caused by blocks within ourselves". He had realised Larry Hirschhorn's truth that leaders and followers *both* contribute to the successes *and* failures of any organisation. When that realization comes, as Michael Lissack (1997) points out, "the managerial challenge is one of asking 'how do I guide and influence?' rather than 'what orders should I give now?'". Collaborative working is the only way around these blocks. At this point also, your understanding of the Meta-model of language, your living of the communication principles in Part 2 and your ability to tell a story and use metaphors, becomes all important. You add another facet to your role – the head as conversational catalyst! Transforming the conversational and collective thinking skills of the people around you to produce a total team ability that is greater than the sum of the individual members' talents.

Shared leadership

"I came to the conclusion that all transformation is tied to personal transformation. The real key is becoming a learner oneself. I continued to recognise that I needed other people to make changes happen, but now I realised that I could not be their teacher. We were all learners together. I had to find a way to lead without having all the answers."

(Peter Negroni, 2000)

125

Schooling has a long history of sole leadership. We have celebrated the charismatic leader and teacher and held them up as the model for others to follow. Perhaps in this millennium, this structure may now be going out of date. Across the world there are examples of alternative approaches to the sole leader. The British National College for School Leadership identified a range of approaches from part-time job-sharing co-head's, through split-task headship, to integrative co-headship and even whole staff leadership collectives (Court, 2003). Carl Rogers developed the idea of group-centred leadership, a basic assumption of which is that it is the relationship between leader and followers which promotes or prevents the development of the learning of the whole group and not the technical or professional expertise of the individuals in it. He advocated that school leaders should take the risk and move the traditional leadership and power boundaries. Leaders in schools are now more psychologically vulnerable than they have ever been – they have to be more open with their colleagues, more open with the community they serve, more open to public scrutiny. Head teachers today have to be prepared to risk the power that traditionally comes with their position, to be better able to develop and lead their team to improve what they do for their learners. In turn, the members of staff have to give up some of their dependency on the head and accept their own leadership role.

So, group-centred leadership means changing the power balance in the school organisation, moving it more towards your colleagues. Creating the conditions in which leadership is distributed throughout the school. A school in which power is shared and professional democracy taken seriously. By taken seriously, I mean working towards the democratic values that the French revolution carried as its *dan tien* – its central aim: liberty, equality, fraternity. Leadership becomes a set of functions which are the property of the group and which can be appropriately shared around the group. Some of the conditions necessary for creating group-centred leadership include setting aside your own agenda and ego and focussing instead on facilitation of the team's growth, the release of its latent creativity and enhancement of its goal achievement. It also means being willing to tackle the emergence of dysfunctional group behaviour – decreasing their dependence on you, breaking up factions, keeping the common task alive and motivating. The set of skills of a group leader may look quite different to many other described sets of competences of effective managers. They include:

- Conveying warmth and empathy by seeing others as valuable by your acceptance of differences.
- Generating trust and authenticity. Genuineness through openness and the establishment of a safe, non-threatening climate. Authenticity – recognising the boundary between those things you can control and those you cannot and not lumping some of the first category into the second category.
- Attending to others – the best leader is the one who is most adaptable to other people's needs.
- Understanding and creating meaning – making coming to school *meaningful* in the lives of staff and students.
- Enabling communication and more – enhancing it through linking the different contributions made by the team. Careful listening to establish the music behind the words can show the congruence between two contributions (the connectedness of which might have been lost either because of the speaker's individual way of expressing themselves or the listener's own hearing filters).

Attaining professional liberty is about increasing the autonomy of the school staff – maximising their level of choice to improve their practice and the school's organisation. In the modern school, as its leader, the more you establish a framework that encourages people to take initiatives within the framework, the more you multiply your own effectiveness by improving the effectiveness of other people. This might mean negotiating goals with your team, problem-setting and solving for themselves. The leader's ultimate objective in such an organisation is to enable group members to fulfil these functions for themselves, independently of the leader. I know that both you as a leader and the staff would find this shift in balance, potentially very threatening and thus, resisted at times by both you and them. Be that as it may, that is your challenge. I believe that trust and commitment levels rise in such an organisation and a climate for learning, growth and change engendered. On taking St. George's School out of its failing state towards success, Marie Stubbs (2003) admitted that "No head is an island, and if I have a secret it is being able to recognise the special qualities in others. My staff have the skills I lack."

Equality translates into equality of opportunity. The opportunity to grow professionally. Research on change in education has identified that schools that have been shown to be learning organisations, are often led by head teachers or principals who have made the increased effectiveness of their staff a key focus for their energy. Truly people-centred leaders who promote the development of each individual's potential in order to change the culture of the school. Leaders who hold higher expectations of their staff, than the staff do of themselves.

For fraternity read collegiality – the only way a school can become a learning organisation is if the staff share their learning about their practice; about the curriculum, about student learning and through joint enquiry, studying what and how they teach.

Working in partnership is becoming more and more important. The head as servant of the school community – "It's not your school – it's our school". The head as servant of the wider community. A town I know has three secondary schools each striving to be centres of excellence in their own right. Although these intentions are to be applauded at one level, at a town-wide level, it has not stopped the attainment of students overall from declining from 5th at infant level out of the seven towns in the region, dropping to 6th at the end of primary schooling and reaching the bottom of the list by the end of the secondary schooling. Would that be different if all three head teachers were jointly accountable to the community's leaders in the town? Would the attainment of the town's children be different if all three head teachers were *jointly responsible* for the education of all the town's children, rather than those that lived in the immediate neighbourhood of each individual school? I believe so. Everyone appreciates that the micro-economic and social differences that occur between neighbourhoods are usually more influential than the quality of individual leadership in their effects on student achievement.

Marian Court (2002) reports on a number of examples of shared leadership of schools across the world: a school in Minnesota USA, in which six out of the school's 28 teachers successfully share the powers of the previous principal; another in New Zealand did so in order to establish a leadership that was 'less focused on trends or the personality of the leader and more on teaching and learning'.

In a restructuring of the Local Education Authority in which I work, the Chief Education Officer decided to amalgamate the four divisional training teams into the department's training arm, working as an independent enterprise unit under a single business manager. I negotiated a structure that kept the four divisional managers as co-equals, managing the business as professional peers, with equal pay and equal status and with shared, but different, responsibilities for its overall success. A tribute to the CEO's willingness to take the risk and break with the traditional hierarchical structure. The unit successfully mounted an annual programme of over 1000 training events and generated a healthy surplus for each year of its five-year existence before the department was restructured yet again!

'Flocking' leadership

In a flock of migrating geese, every individual takes its turn at being the front flier at some point in the flock's migration. For professional growth, everybody in a school should have the opportunity to lead at some time or other – and if everyone needs to be leader, then everyone also needs to be a follower. The appropriate leader will depend on the task, whether it is an area of curriculum development, staff development, team building, project management, strategic planning or budget management. The leader is either the person most skilful in the task area or the person who needs the opportunity to develop the requisite skills. In the first case, the followers have the tasks of supporting their current leader and in the second, giving the learning leader firstly, space to experiment and secondly, providing them with constructive feedback on their leadership.

Captain Kirk was always an 'up-front' leader, always beaming down to lead his team in the trouble spots of the worlds he visited. His successor, Captain Picard, rarely does so – he usually delegates and delegates well, often saving whole civilisations through the achievements of others! A sure sign of when you succeed as a mature head in really giving the up-front leadership away, is the intense feeling you may experience of desperately wanting it back and wanting to beam yourself right into the centre of the action. Look out for it and then resist the urge. And then congratulate yourself! You have crossed the galaxy and arrived at your ideal landing ground – successful headship.

The Final Frontier
To boldly go...

As he stepped out onto the moon, Neil Armstrong didn't forget the many, many steps that preceded his own "Just one small step...". So, knowing about the importance of many small steps, in arriving at a giant leap, I have included some small steps to conclude this guide to the space and time exploration of headship. The principles you have just read are just words on paper. They have to be converted into deeds.

Now you can put the principles into action. You can do this by taking the time to practise each one of the principles in turn and then begin to notice the effects they have on your leadership. Don't be eager to take the giant leap, yet. Just know that it will come. These particular exercises in using the principles are steps you can take in the safety of your own home. Rehearsing them out of context and rehearsing them in context is the way to learn. When you are able to rehearse good processes, you can achieve excellent performance.

I am not going to say you can live up to all these principles right away...

However...

you can make a start on turning them into reality for you as you do the following exercises.

Walking in space

This is where you can utilise all the principles. Firstly, think of a situation or an issue in school which you have not handled as well as you know you could have. Take one or more of the principles that you think might have helped you, and then personalise each one in turn, as though it is now a belief of yours. Reconsider the situation in the light of this belief. Then the next and the next and so on.

Let me give you a push start

...let's say you have had a difficult exchange with a member of staff... or a parent... or a child...

Recapture the situation, then say to yourself:

1. *Behaviour is the best form of information about a person*
    What is the behaviour telling you? When you have considered your answer to that, move on to the next principle, then the next, and so on to the end.

2. *This person's behaviour is the best choice available to him/her just now*
    There are times when we do not know the extent of our own resourcefulness. We then act in a limited way, in what seems our only way. What resources does the other person have that he/she is blind to just now? What has it done to your understanding of the situation, now that you can see that his/her behaviour was his/her best choice?

3. *This person's behaviour is well-intentioned at some level*
    Look at the behaviour from the other person's point of view. Stand in their shoes. What could the positive intention of the behaviour be?

4. *This person is responding to their map of the world, not mine*
    Just what is this person's world like right now? How might their mindscape be shaping this behaviour?

5. *This person is not just this behaviour*
   This person behaves quite differently in other circumstances. This person is more than just this behaviour.

6. *There are no resistant colleagues, just inflexible communicators*
   If we are not communicating, just how am I stuck in my own response? What can I do differently?

After these six principles, consider how you view the situation now. Do you feel more resourceful yourself? Do you have a number of options for exploring the situation, now?

(This exercise is often more powerful if you stand in the middle of the room and imagine the principles located on stones set as a circle around you – much like planets around a sun. The centre represents your problem space and you can step out of the centre and on to a principle space – a different planet – and turn to look back at the problem with the specific principle in mind. Notice how the issue appears to you in the light of the principle. Then move back in to the centre and notice how you feel about it now.)

(Adapted from an exercise developed by Robert Dilts and used with kind permission of the author.)

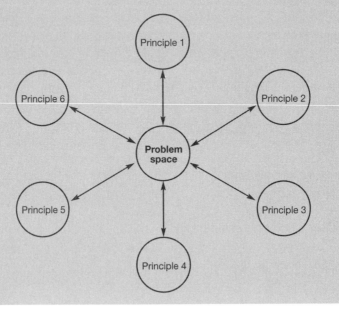

Six steps to the heavens

Now you can integrate all your learning from this book. You can carry the principles you have adopted and layer on to them everything else you have acquired from this book. You can use your heightened awareness *with* your better emotional management *and* wider analytical and thinking skills, *while* appreciating the deeper structure of the language people use, to develop more flexible behaviour. Start by giving yourself enough space to take half a dozen unimpeded steps. Place six sheets of paper a pace apart or imagine there are six stepping-stones across the floor of the room. Each one represents the different aspects of your role as a head teacher. Answer the questions at the first space then step onto the next, answer the questions for that space and so on. When you get to the sixth space turn around and retrace your steps, answering the questions for each space again, in turn. Notice the difference on the way back.

1. **The environment space**
   Think about the environment in which you work, notice what you can see around you, and listen to the sounds you hear from it. The feelings you have about the place.

   * *Where do you lead?*
   * *When do you lead?*

   When you have written down answers to these two questions, step forward one pace.

2. **The behaviour space**
   Take a moment to think about your behaviour in the school.

   * *What are you good at as a head teacher?*
   * *What do you do as a head teacher?* (be specific)

   Once again, when you are ready move forward one more pace.

3. **The capability space**
   Now think about your skills, those you have already and those you have acquired in reading this book.

   * *How do you want to lead staff?*
   * *What can you do as a leader?*
   * *What are you capable of as a leader?*

4. **The beliefs and values space**
   Think about what you would like to believe is possible.

   - *What do you believe about yourself as a head teacher?*
   - *What does that say about you?*
   - *What must be true for you to be able to say that?*

   Notice how your beliefs have changed since reading this book.

5. **The identity space**
   Think about this unique person you are. There is no other head teacher like you. Think about how you express your uniqueness about what you really want to do and then answer the one question.

   - *Who are you as a head teacher?*

6. **The community space**
   Create a symbol, an emblem or a badge to represent your relationship as a head teacher to the staff and the wider school community.

   - *What would it be?*

   Now when you are ready take this symbol of your linkage to the wider community with you, step back into your identity space.

Answer the identity questions anew.

Then take the enriched sense of yourself back into the beliefs and values space. Once again re-answer the questions for this space. Answer these and move on.

Answers going forward

1 _____

2 _____

3 _____

4 _____

5 _____

6 _____

When you are ready, move back to your capability space and become aware how your new view of your beliefs and values allow you to do the things that satisfy you and others. Continue on answering the questions and stepping back until you arrive back at the starting space.

(Adapted from an exercise developed by Robert Dilts and used with kind permission of the author.)

Answers coming back

1 _____

2 _____

3 _____

4 _____

5 _____

6 _____

Words into action

The four pillars of wisdom

All good action is founded on four axioms:

1. *Know what you want, what outcome you seek and that it is beneficial*
    As a formal leader, you carry a huge responsibility for your choice of outcomes. You can choose them to be good in the light of equality, human relationships and community benefit.

2. *Be flexible enough in your choice of behaviour to get it*
    To be really skilful means to be able to choose from your total repertoire of behaviours, those that you need to deploy to achieve your goals. Ethically doing what you have to do to gain the outcome. Deciding whether you can alter your own mindscape sufficiently to achieve the goal means seeking the resources within yourself to extend your capabilities beyond what you once believed were their outer limits.

3. *Choose it and do it*
    You do actually have to take action and do something different to gain a different outcome. This guide can take you only so far. Like all travel guides you will know when to put it down and get on with fully experiencing the place you are in now. Then, you can be free to go and explore your future.

4. *Have sufficient awareness of what is going on around you to know when you have got it*
    Some people carry on travelling after they have arrived at their destination. They keep deploying past successful behaviours beyond the point of appropriateness.

Be aware of when you have arrived and stop and enjoy the view.

Recommended reading for the journey

The Known Universe

Adams, D., 1994, *The Hitchhiker's Guide To The Galaxy, Millennium Edition,* Orion Books, London, UK.

Adams, D., 1994, *The Restaurant At The End Of The Universe, Millennium Edition,* Orion Books, London, UK.

Adams, D., 1994, *Life, The Universe And Everything, Millennium Edition,* Orion Books, London, UK.

Bach, R., 1973, *Jonathan Livingston Seagull,* Pan Books, London, UK.

Bandler, R., 1993, *Time For A Change,* Meta Publications, California, USA.

Bateson, G., 1973, *Information, Form And Substance,* In: *Steps To An Ecology Of Mind,* Paladin, England, UK.

Day, C., Hall, C., Gammage, P. and Coles, M., 1993, *Leadership And Curriculum In The Primary School,* Paul Chapman Publishing, London, UK.

Elliot, J., 1991, *Action Research For Educational Change,* Open University Press, Bucks., UK.

Feynman, P., 1986, *Surely, You're Joking Mr. Feynman!: Adventures Of A Curious Character,* Unwin, London, UK.

Fisher, R. and Ury, W., 1981, *Getting To Yes,* Arrow Business Books, London, UK.

Fullan, M., 1992, *What's Worth Fighting For In Headship,* Open University Press, Bucks., UK.

Fullan, M., 1999, *Change Forces: the sequel,* Falmer Press, Philadelphia, PA.

Gardner, H., 1983, *Frames Of Mind: The Theory Of Multiple Intelligences,* Basic Books, NY, USA.

Goleman, D., 1996, *Emotional Intelligence: Why It Matters More Than IQ*, Bloomsbury, London, UK.

Grinder, J. and Bandler, R., 1975, *The Structure Of Magic II: A Book About Communication And Change*, Science and Behaviour Books, Palo Alto, California, USA.

Hall, V., 1996, *Dancing On The Ceiling: A Study Of Women Managers In Education*, Paul Chapman Publishing, London, UK.

Heron, J., 1989, *The Facilitator's Handbook*, Kogan Page, London, UK.

Hirschhorn, L., 1997, *Reworking Authority: Leading And Following In The Post-Modern Organization*, Cambridge, MIT Press, Massachusetts, USA.

House of Commons, 1998, *The Role of Head Teachers*, Select Committee On Education And Employment, 9th Report, London, UK.

Jackins, H., 1965, *The Human Side Of Human Beings*, Rational Island Publishers, Seattle, USA.

Leithwood, D., Begley, P. and Cousins, B., 1994, *Developing Expert Leadership For Future Schools*, Falmer Press, London, UK.

Loader, D., 1997, *The Inner Principle*, Falmer Press, London, UK.

MacGilchrist, B., Myers, K. and Reed, J., 1997, *The Intelligent School*, Paul Chapman Publishing, London, UK.

Marinaccio, D., 1998, *All The Other Things I Really Need To Know I Learned From Watching Star Trek: The Next Generation*, Pocket Books, N.Y., USA.

McClelland, D.C., 1961, *The Achieving Society*, Van Nostrand, N. Y., USA.

Morgan, G., 1986, *Images Of Organisations*, Sage Publications, London, UK.

Negroni, P., 2000, *The Superintendent's Progress*, In: Senge, P., Cambron-McCabe, N. H., Lucas, T., Smith, B., Dutton, J. and Kleiner, A. (Eds), 2000, *Schools That Learn*, Nicholas Brealey, London, pp.425-432.

Pearson, C.S., 1998, *The Hero Within: Six Archetypes We Live By*, Harper, San Francisco, USA.

Perls, F.S., 1969, *Gestalt Therapy Verbatim*, Real People Press, Moab, Utah, USA.

Pinker, S., 1994, *The Language Instinct: A New Science Of Language And Mind*, Penguin, London, UK.

Rogers, C., 1983, *Freedom To Learn For The 80s*, Merrill, Columbus, Ohio, USA.

Schon, D., 1983, *The Reflective Practitioner*, Temple Smith, London, UK.

Senge, P., 1990, *The Fifth Discipline*, Century Business, London, UK.

Straangard, F., 1981, *NLP Made Visual*, Connector, Copenhagen.

Teacher Training Agency, 1997, *National Standards For Head Teachers*, Dept. for Education and Employment, England, UK.

Stubbs, M., 2003, *Ahead of the Class*, John Murray, London.

West, S., 1993, *Educational Values for School Leadership*, Kogan Page, London, UK.

The Expanding Frontier

Atkinson and Claxton, G. (eds), 2000, *The Intuitive Practitioner: on the value of not always knowing what one is doing*, Open University, Buckingham, England.

Bryner A. and Markova, D., 1997, *An Unused Intelligence; Physical Thinking For 21st Century Leadership*, Conari Press, Berkeley, California, USA.

Claxton, G., 1997, *Hare Brain, Tortoise Mind: Why Intelligence Increases When You Think* Less, Fourth Estate, London, UK.

Court, M., 2003, *Different Approaches to Sharing School Leadership*: *International Research Associate Perspectives*, National College for School Leadership, Nottingham, England.

Elliott, J., 1991, *Action Research for Educational Change (Developing Teachers and Teaching)*, Open University Press, Maidenhead, Berkshire.

Dilts, R., 2003, *From Coach to Awakener*, Meta Publications, Capitola, California, USA.

Dilts, R. and Bonissone, G., 1991, *Skills Of The Future*, Meta Publications, Capitola, California, USA.

Dryden, G. and Voss, J., 1994, *The Learning Revolution*, Accelerated Learning Systems, Aylesbury, Bucks., UK.

Fullan, M., 1993, *Change Forces: Probing the Depths of Educational Reform*, Falmer Press, London, UK.

Jensen, E., 1994, *The Learning Brain*, Turning Point, San Diego, California, USA.

Lissack, M.R., 1997, *Metaphor and Art: Organisational Sensemaking and Yasmina Reza's Play*, Warsaw, Poland: Presentation to the 15th International SCOS Conference.

McDermott, I. and Shircore, I., 1999, *Manage Yourself, Manage Your Life*, Piatkus, London, UK.

Porter, P.K., 1993, *Awaken The Genius: Mind Technology For The 21st Century*, Awaken the Genius Foundation, Virginia Beach, Va., USA.

Ritzer, G., 1996, *The McDonaldisation of Society*, Pine Forge, California, USA.

Pinker, S., 1997, *How The Mind Works*, Allen Lane, London, UK.

Cyber-space-stations

I welcome discussion and comments on any aspect of this book and can be contacted on: terry.omahony@hants.gov.uk

Further information and sources of books, articles, events and training on neuro-linguistic programming in education can be found on the World Wide Web at such sites as:

Anglo-American Book Company Ltd:
http://www.anglo-american.co.uk

Association for NLP:
http://anlp.org

Education network:
http://new-oceans.co.uk/ednet

International Teaching Seminars:
http://www.nlp.community.com

Robert Dilts:
http://www.nlpu.com

Index

USA & Canada *orders to:*
Crown House Publishing
P.O. Box 2223, Williston, VT 05495-2223, USA
Tel: 877-925-1213, Fax: 802-864-7626
E-mail: info@CHPUS.com
www.CHPUS.com

UK & Rest of World *orders to:*
The Anglo American Book Company Ltd.
Crown Buildings, Bancyfelin, Carmarthen, Wales SA33 5ND
Tel: +44 (0)1267 211880/211886, Fax: +44 (0)1267 211882
E-mail: books@anglo-american.co.uk
www.anglo-american.co.uk

Australasia *orders to:*
Footprint Books Pty Ltd.
Unit 4/92A Mona Vale Road, Mona Vale NSW 2103, Australia
Tel: +61 (0) 2 9997 3973, Fax: +61 (0) 2 9997 3185
E-mail: info@footprint.com.au
www.footprint.com.au

Singapore *orders to:*
Publishers Marketing Services Pte Ltd.
10-C Jalan Ampas #07-01
Ho Seng Lee Flatted Warehouse, Singapore 329513
Tel: +65 6256 5166, Fax: +65 6253 0008
E-mail: info@pms.com.sg
www.pms.com.sg

Malaysia *orders to:*
Publishers Marketing Services Pte Ltd
Unit 509, Block E, Phileo Damansara 1, Jalan 16/11
46350 Petaling Jaya, Selangor, Malaysia
Tel : 03 7955 3588, Fax : 03 7955 3017
E-mail: pmsmal@po.jaring.my
www.pms.com.sg

South Africa *orders to:*
Everybody's Books
Box 201321 Durban North 401, 1 Highdale Road,
25 Glen Park, Glen Anil 4051, KwaZulu NATAL, South Africa
Tel: +27 (0) 31 569 2229, Fax: +27 (0) 31 569 2234
E-mail: ebbooks@iafrica.com